ISBN-13: 9798399115504
ISBN-10: 1477123456

Cover design by: Art Painter
Library of Congress Control Number: 2018675309
Printed in the United States of America

THE UNDERDOG TRAVELS BEFORE BRENDAN

THE RIVETINGLY EXCITING PREQUEL TO
underdogs

By Gray Freeman

One man sets off in a van on a voyage of self-discovery - to fulfil a dream and travel around the coast of Britain. *Without a dog!* What *was* he thinking?

ABOUT THE AUTHOR

Gray Freeman is a writer and traveller – and often a travel writer. He lives in south Manchester with his dog, Brendan - he came with his name. He sits and writes stuff and then takes his dog for a walk.

BY GRAY FREEMAN

The underdogs series:
0. the underdog
1. underdogs
2. DOG DAYS: underdogs 2
3: underdogs 3 (COMING SOON {ISH})

Also available:
THE LONG GOODBYE and Other Plays

CONTENTS

FOREWORD

I am one of the writers of the *underdogs* series, in which I have travelled - and sometimes stayed at home - with my dog, Brendan. In our first book, the appropriately titled *underdogs,* we met and went on a roadtrip around the coast of England. But before this - before I met Brendan - probably while he was still a street dog in Bulgaria, I began my trip alone. It had long been an ambition to travel around the coast of Britain in a campervan, seeing new places, having experiences, sitting and watching the sun set over the sea, strolling along deserted beaches at twilight and eating cake. Probably quite a bit of the latter.

But life got in the way, work got in the way, then suddenly I wasn't working anymore and I had time on my hands. I wanted a life change and I hoped this trip would reveal to me my new path.

You might be tempted to think this was a midlife crisis - and that would be a very plausible reason; I was definitely stricken with midlife and I have never strayed far from a crisis. I'd love it if it was a rebellious reaction to getting older, but it wasn't really anything to do with my age, it was just something I wanted to do and something I needed to do. It was the trip itself that mattered, more than the destination. I could canoe the length of the Amazon – which was a river before it was an online retailer – or I could trek the Himalayas, but why should I bother, when I had Britain, quite literally, on my doorstep, and – according to the blurb – it was *Great*.

As we live on an island, it seems almost churlish not to travel around the perimeter at some point. It was something I'd always wanted to do, always *intended* to do, but I never had. There was always something stopping me: commitments, headlines, deadlines, breadlines. Well, not any more! It was time to seize the day and make things happen!

I had a campervan, which in recent years had just become a vehicle to drive to work in. Now, without work it was a campervan again. It was Eagle One; it was my escape vehicle. I was going off on a great adventure, a voyage of discovery, self-discovery and exploration. And the really great news was that I would never be very far away from my own kettle!

So, that was the beginning; I was setting off travelling, alone. I have never had a problem being alone and enjoy my own company. I had no dog in my life and I didn't want one. I enjoyed the freedom that not having a dog allowed me. Meanwhile, Brendan would probably have been buying and selling on the black market, wheeling and dealing and generally up to no good. Anyway, that's another story for another time.

Gray Freeman.

CHAPTER 1: NORTH BY NORTHWEST

In which I start my circumnavigation of Britain... and end up vomiting into a carrier bag.

So, it's midnight and I'm driving north in Eagle One, my trusty camper van. At parties, she boasts she's a four berth, but it's merely a drunken lie; she's just large enough for one person, if you pack light and enjoy being cramped. (The pull-out "double bed" is five-foot square. I'm six foot four, so whichever way I lie, it's just too small.) But she's mine and I have everything I need at my fingertips.

My world is as far as the yellow beam of the headlights: there's nothing else. This is Day One and I'm filled with excitement and anticipation. To counter any wayward positivity, I'm listening to the Smiths. I don't know why I chose the Smiths, but they're Mancunian and I'm leaving Manchester, so I suppose it just seems appropriate.

I enjoy travelling. I don't really like *driving*, but I enjoy being on a trip. Often the journey is more important than the destination. The journey crackles with anticipation and the excitement of what lies ahead, whereas the destination can sometimes be disappointing and an anti-climax.

The outward journey is odd; you're travelling towards somewhere, but you're also travelling away from home, away from the things you know, away from people. I miss my partner, Nicky, most on the first day, especially on the journey. She'll be at home asleep now with her cats. We don't live together. We did; we don't now. Usually this rather empty feeling of missing only dissipates after I've had a brew, so I stop at Lancaster services.

I've only been driving an hour, but it feels longer. The services are partly closed at this time and many of the shops inside are dark and shuttered. The toilets are weirdly empty; the row of urinals completely, vacantly and hauntingly still. They suddenly flush automatically and needlessly. No one's weed in here for hours.

I stand at the counter of a well-known brand of coffee emporium upstairs in the services. Despite the late hour it's still open – allegedly – though there don't appear to be any staff and there are cakes on display that are at risk of becoming a permanent feature. I wait patiently – patiently-ish – for several minutes, looking at the strip lights and the plastic floor tiles, then I notice the tubby assistant rising slowly on the escalator. He sees me but makes no acknowledgement and makes no attempt to quicken his pace. I smile at him, expecting a friendly apology: "Sorry, I just nipped off to do an errand because it was so quiet." or something similar, but nothing. He serves me grudgingly and manages to create one of the foulest coffees I've ever tasted.

Back outside, I pour my coffee away. There are lots of lorries in the lorry park opposite, but no sign of anyone in them, sleeping or otherwise. I would expect to see at least some of them with a flickering glow from the driver in his bed watching *Carry On Up the Khyber* on his iPad, or combing his beard, or whatever truckers do at night. But nothing.

I'm starting to get a tiredness headache, so I decide to lie down and have forty winks. As an experiment, I actually *do* forty winks... It's rubbish; I don't feel refreshed at all. In fact, if anything it increases my headache. I doze fitfully, but it isn't very relaxing. I stay in the services for the permitted two hours and then reluctantly power up the Smiths and head back to the M6; that ribbon of orange light cutting through the darkness, heading ever-northwards.

The last leg is over the Shap moors, between Kendal and Carlisle. There's no view whatsoever, just bands of thick, impenetrable fog, which makes it an exciting drive, out in the middle of nowhere, totally alone... apart from the seven hundred and twenty-eight huge and slow-moving lorries that I'm sandwiched between. I come to the final services available to me and bed down again. Tiredness overcoming my excitement...

* * * * * * * * * *

I've just opened my eyes and I'm chilled to the bone, my clothes are sticking to me with an icy dampness and I feel more tired now than before I went to sleep. It's starting to get light, which can't be right... I realise I must have fallen into a deep sleep and slept through my two-hour alarm. I've overstayed my permitted time in the car park, so I speed off immediately and drive into Carlisle.

Morrissey had warned me that there was panic on the streets of Carlisle, but he was over-reacting, as usual. Carlisle is actually rather sedate, soporific even; there aren't currently enough people around to create a panic… or even form a Barbershop Quartet.

I had come across an interesting website called "The Knowhere Guide", which compiles lists of facts and opinions – and libel mainly – about places, sent in by the public. Reasons to avoid Carlisle include: "lots of nonces", "the accent", "Chavs, Nazis and teenies with no brain". Although I was born in city centre Manchester ("rain", "crime", "beggars") I have lived all my life in Stockport, so was curious to see what people didn't like about my hometown. ("Scallies", "scallys", "traffic lights", "chavz", "chavs" and "skallies".) I don't think that's very fair on traffic lights. The Knowhere Guide is going to be fun!

Regardless of Carlisle's alleged "Chavs, Nazis and teenies with no brain", it turns out to be a handsome city. It has wide, cobbled Georgian streets and some lovely old buildings. It's still so quiet. I check the time. It's barely 7am on a bitterly cold morning; only a few early workers and the most conscientious seagulls are up and about. I go to look at the castle. Unfortunately, it's closed. I go to look at the cathedral. Unfortunately, it's closed. I go to look at the old court. Unfortunately, it's closed. I go into Costa for a coffee. Unfortunately, it's open.

I drink my Americano as slowly as possible, trying to make the experience last, then I step back out into the cold and pace the streets until Carlisle slowly begins to open. Gratefully, I duck into bookshops and charity shops like a rough sleeper looking for warmth; the brief blasts of hot air from overdoor heaters is bliss. After I've exhausted my list of things to do in a virtually closed city, I return to Eagle One and leave Carlisle. (Eventually. It's easier to get into than out of.)

* * * * * * * * * *

I'm heading west, towards the coast. I pause briefly in Burgh-on-sands, a very attractive village, but not twee; it's solidly built, real stone, old handmade bricks and wooden beams. It has a fortified church built on the site of a Roman fort. The tower is like a castle keep, strengthened to offer protection to the villagers from the marauding Scottish Scots – who came across the nearby Solway Firth - from Scotland – in search of trouble and sticky toffee pudding.

Soon after Burgh, the road runs along the course of Hadrian's Wall – a big wall built by the Emperor Hadrian to keep those marauding Scots out. It seems the poor Scots are infamous for their marauding and have been for a very long time. The building of the wall began in AD122 and it defined the northern-most limit of the Roman Empire. The Romans had conquered most of Europe, but they stopped short of tackling the Scots – possibly due to their reputation for marauding. Remarkably, Hadrian's Wall is the largest Roman artefact *in the world*. Contrary to popular belief, it has never marked the boundary between England and Scotland and exists completely in England, though it does run close to the border at times on its 73-mile length.

Across a wide expanse of salt marshes, I can see the tidal estuary of the Solway Firth, which *does* serve as part of the border between the two countries. Across the water, Scotland looks like... anywhere really... mainly hills and fields and little white dots which are houses. At one time, the estuary near here was crossed by an iron railway viaduct. After the railway closed, the bridge was used as a footpath, popular with those formerly-marauding Scots, who marched over for Sunday drinking – as Scottish law forbade it – then staggered home in the wee small hours. The viaduct was demolished in the early 'Thirties and the thirsty Scots had to make other drinking arrangements.

Continuing along the coast road, I pass through various other villages and hamlets, but none of them are as pleasing as Burgh-on-sands; they are practical, angular, solidly built to withstand the salt winds. One of these hard, no-nonsense estuary villages is Port Carlisle, which was linked by canal to the city from which it takes its name. The canal was closed in Victorian times and the port silted up. The various villages look insular; you can imagine that very little has changed here for centuries. I'm not saying they *do* practice the black arts in these isolated little places, but you could certainly believe that they might.

The landscape quite surprises me, as it isn't the sort I associate with Cumbria. It's mainly flat, criss-crossed with drainage channels, ditches, banks and hump-backed bridges; it makes me think of the Fens. Whilst not the picture postcard countryside of the Lake District, it's certainly still very green and pastoral.

In the early afternoon, I arrive in the little seaside town of Silloth, situated on the Firth. It prides itself on being "a small town with a very big heart". Over-sized organs aside, apart from a hideous industrial estate on the approach, the town seems very pleasant. Silloth has been known since Victorian times for the "quality of its air" and I can confirm it has plenty. The houses on the main street are Regency-style and colourfully painted and Silloth seems so relaxed, bordering on the downright lazy.

I book in on the nearest (and only) campsite, which is much, *much* more expensive than I'm really happy to pay, but I want to ensure I have a good night's sleep. It's an achingly respectable, Daily-Mail-under-the-arm sort of place. I have tinned veg curry for tea and then set off for a walk along the beach, towards the end of the tapering peninsula, which juts into the Firth. I'm walking along slowly just enjoying the scenery, enjoying the sharp sea breeze, enjoying being here – somewhere I've never been before. It's quite blissful.

I wander along the shore as the sun is sinking low over the sea. The tide is out and the beach is muddy sand and rough stones. Over the estuary, curlews are calling, a lonesome and haunting cry.

I always find this a rather poignant time, between day and night. Twilight is a time for winding down. Something about the dwindling sunshine always makes me rather reflective. I've been busy all day, completely occupied, but at sundown it's very easy to feel lonely. Sunset is a time to be with your partner, but - as the sun melts into the watery horizon – I'm all alone. Apart from the curlews. The sun sinks unceremoniously into the sea; there isn't even any steam. It suddenly becomes very cold, so I return to my van, realising too late that I am re-entering the site without a Daily Mail or Express under my arm, and that will surely be frowned upon by my curtain-twitching, middle-class neighbours in their luxury caravans, with their levelling blocks, rotary washing lines, solar fairy lights and satellite dishes.

I'm looking forward to jumping into bed and falling into a deep sleep. As it happens, I do neither of these things. Any "jumping into bed" has to be pre-planned, as pulling the bed out takes several minutes, a fair amount of effort and a good degree of swearing. When I finally *do* jump in, the feeling of sleepiness has long since passed, so I lie awake for ages listening to the ceaseless, strained pitch of the North Sea wind.

* * * * * * * * * *

When you're on a campsite, you know it's morning, not when the cock crows, but when you hear the deep rumbling of the first sewage cartridges being wheeled to the chemical toilet disposal point. They get up at the crack of dawn to do it, as though the drain is going to get full if they're not there early enough. It's always the man's job. Middle-aged and older men converge from all areas of the site, wearing corduroy trousers and baseball caps, dragging what looks like a shopping trolley, except it's not full of bargains from Aldi. This noise – rubber wheels on concrete – pulls me into consciousness in the early, icy morning.

It's a dull, grey morning, not very inspiring. I have a tea then lie down again for an hour, worrying that I'm not having a good enough experience. (This kind of negative, paranoid, time-wasting cynicism is the best character assessment for me you could ask for.) I'd had a great(ish) day yesterday; I've never set off anywhere at midnight before, I've never slept in services, I've never walked around Carlisle at 7am in the freezing, white light of morning – or at any time or in any temperature, for that matter. I'd seen some new places, but I hadn't come to any life-changing decisions.

I decide – eventually – that this is a voyage of discovery and any revelations will come naturally; my epiphany will unfold when the time is right. Holding on to that thought, I get dressed and drive off, past other people's caravans, past other people's homes, past other people's washing blowing in other people's wind.

The roads in the centre of Silloth aren't very well-signed and I end up driving round and round the area of the docks, which is something you can get a reputation for. I try every turning until, by chance, I find the exit road. At the next junction though, a sign declares the coastal route is closed due to roadworks. I follow diversion signs, leading me off inland, I know not where. I pass through a flat landscape dotted with wind turbines, through a lot of villages which are all pebble-dashed, depressing and as grey as the suffocating sky above. I wonder if it's the bad weather making them appear so grim and despairing, but at 11.30 the sun comes out briefly and I see grey pebble-dashing in sunshine – still just as depressing.

I arrive in Maryport, once an important ship-building centre, so - not surprisingly - it has an ocean-going feel; many of the roads and fixtures have nautical names: Shipping Brow, the Lifeboat Inn, the Captain Nelson pub and Christian Street, named after Fletcher Christian, ringleader of the mutiny on *The Bounty*, who was born nearby. Christian set Captain Bligh adrift in a rowing boat, due to his harsh treatment of the crew. Captain Bligh wasn't best pleased.

Maryport's high street isn't unattractive, with Georgian and Victorian houses and shops. Several people are standing at the corners of streets, seemingly waiting to cross, but when the traffic stops they just remain standing there. I realise they aren't actually pedestrians; this is just how they pass their time.

It's blowing a gale and beginning to rain. I stroll around the docks, which would once have been teeming with life, but now seem sad and full of rusting keels and the decaying remains of a large boat. "Frigate." I think, then I leave Maryport.

* * * * * * * * * * *

I drive along an A-road through Flimby – which sounds a bit like a Cold War spy. Ahead is an evil-looking factory, like a monumental castle with tubes and turrets. I'm still listening to the Smiths as I let the by-pass lead me around the edges of industrial Workington. "The rain falls hard on a humdrum town." Morrissey tells me. "This town has dragged you down." He's not wrong.

Workington ("no money and no slappers", "the fukin cops" (sic), "It's like the town that time forgot, this is the worst place ever.") was a coal and steel town. When those industries declined Workington became an unemployment blackspot. Today, millions have been poured into regenerating the town centre and it looks quite impressive at high speed.

I drive up into the hills above Saint Bees, the most westerly point of Cumbria. I find a small carpark in an old farmyard. A crudely fashioned sign reads: £2 All Day. There is an elderly man loitering in a ragged and creaking tin barn. He keeps looking over, but is trying to pretend he isn't, by earnestly feigning being hard at work. It's clear he's waiting to see if I'm going to pay. I'm not sure if he's the car park attendant, which seems a bit pointless, as at maximum fillage it could only hold about three cars. He doesn't come over and I want to put him out of his misery, so I approach him with a smile and ask where or who I should pay.

"There's an honesty box over there…" He points vaguely, dismissively. "Or you can pay me, if you want to!" he adds with much more gusto. Clearly the second option is his preference.

I reluctantly hand him a hard-earned two-pound coin, which he seizes and stows quickly, furtively upon his person. He looks at my boots and asks if I'm going to do some climbing. I laugh and say a firm "No." He then looks up at the sky and scratches his grey stubble thoughtfully, the way that country folk do in fiction, as though he knows the ways of the land, the sea and sky, the lore of nature, the old ways, the rhyme and reason, the changing seasons, the secrets of the hedgerows, the language of the sparrows, the rhythm of life – which apparently has a powerful beat. He doesn't actually lick a finger and hold it up, but he looks like he really wants to. He seems very apologetic about the weather: the upshot is that it's bad and going to stay bad. He's sorry and regretful, but I don't hold him responsible. "Well, have a nice walk." he says, his weather rumination complete. And with that – and my two-pound coin – he jumps into a tractor and speeds off down a stony driveway.

As the dust settles, I set off along a track between farmed fields, which leads towards the sea. It's blustery and very cold, with a salty dampness to the air. There's a huge tractor ploughing a field; in another field there is the little tractor of The Forecasting Farmer, seemingly just parked there, doing nothing. I think I've worked out the situation here: the old chap in the little tractor has had to step aside for his son in the big alpha-male tractor. The old man is probably a widower – and probably lives with his son and family in the farmhouse that was once his own. He does some light work, more for *his* benefit than because he's needed: tinkering in the tin barn, pottering in the potting shed and the occasional weather readings. He has basically been usurped, emasculated and is now redundant. I feel sorry for him, yet he still gets to shoot around in a little tractor and take people's money, like a farming version of Dick Turpin, so it isn't all bad.

I catch my first glimpse of the proper open sea, rather than a tidal estuary. The horizon is out of focus, the sea and the sky are just varying shades of grey. On a good day you can allegedly see as far as the Isle of Man, but there's no chance of that today.

I come to the small, squat tower of Saint Bee's lighthouse. It's in a fine location, suitably exposed and isolated, no other building for some distance. I'd love to sit in the lamp room on a stormy night looking out over the brooding seascape. I take way too many photographs and then continue along the cliff path, towards Whitehaven, far below. Whitehaven ("inbred locals they love jam" (sic), "All the smackheads", "everything. It's awful. Please stay away.") was once one of the major ports in Britain and a centre for ship building. We're going to hear a near-identical CV for virtually every other coastal town, so brace yourself.

* * * * * * * * * * *

In June 2010, the area hit the headlines in the worst possible way, when a local man, 52-year-old taxi driver, Derrick Bird, went on a shooting spree and killed twelve people, injuring another eleven. It was one of the worst criminal acts involving firearms in British history. The police from nearby Sellafield assisted the regular constabulary with the subsequent manhunt which resulted in Derrick Bird turning his gun upon himself.

I say "nearby" Sellafield, though on my Ordnance Survey map, the controversial nuclear plant isn't actually mentioned by name, it is listed simply as "works", even though the nearest railway station is called Sellafield, which sort of gives it away. It's a rambling complex, as big as a small Lakeland town. I find it quite bizarre that every individual building on the site is shown on the map, along with driveways and roads; this would surely be more help to anyone up to no good than simply using the name. If you were a serious terrorist or eco-warrior, you would know exactly where the plant was and these half-hearted attempts to sabotage you by the OS wouldn't put you off.

At one time, Sellafield was a small rural community,

but in the late 'Forties, the British government decided to develop weapons of an atom-splitting nature and the Sellafield site – then known as Windscale – was selected to provide spent fuel rods, needed for the manufacture of nuclear weapons.

Coincidentally, Morrissey is cheerfully singing from my speakers: "If it's not love, then it's the bomb that will bring us together." I'm not sure I agree with his thinking. Another line from his pen keeps running through my head: "Last night the plans for a future war were all I saw on Channel 4." Although the words were written in the 'Eighties, they are so relevant today, regarding the present North Korea situation. As I drive around the coast, Kim Jong-un is threatening global destruction with his shiny new arsenal of nuclear toys. Donald Trump is flinging insults and counter-threats back. A nuclear deterrent – the threat of "mutually assured destruction" (acronym: MAD) – can only work if all participants are sane. In this case I don't think that applies to *any* of the players.

Sellafield is famous. Probably more *infamous*. In 1956, Calder Hall – part of the complex – became the first nuclear power station in Britain to generate electricity on a commercial scale. Sellafield has been notoriously likened to a "nuclear laundry", accepting the radioactive soiled sheets of the world to reprocess and dispose of. Unfortunately, even after you've rinsed it under the tap, nuclear waste is surprisingly toxic and a pain to dispose of safely.

In 1981, while Duran Duran were pouting in eye-liner, the Windscale plant was renamed Sellafield, officially due to restructuring; unofficially to try and disassociate it in the public consciousness from negative reports about its safety: a ploy that didn't entirely work. There have been numerous other serious incidents or accidents involving "off-site radiological releases", as well as deliberate discharges into the atmosphere and into the Irish Sea. Greenpeace claim that this section of ocean remains one of the most heavily contaminated seas in the world.

Perhaps most damning of all, in 1999 it was discovered that Sellafield staff had been falsifying fuel quality data. In February 2005, it was reported that nearly 30 kilograms of plutonium was unaccounted for during auditing. The same year, there was a radioactive waste leak, which resulted in a fine, like you get when your library books are late back.

The Sellafield site houses "the most hazardous industrial building in western Europe". As if that's not kudos enough, it also houses "the *second* most hazardous industrial building in western Europe" as well! They are known as Building B30 and Building B38 respectively. This revelation really put Sellafield on the map. Just not the Ordnance Survey map.

* * * * * * * * * * *

The village of Ravenglass was built at the confluence of three rivers, the Irt, Esk and Mite. It was once a very prosperous port until the estuary silted up. The old village has one main street with a mixture of dwellings, from poky two-up, two-downs to detached Georgian villas. It's odd to see them side by side, but they make a very pleasingly eclectic mix.

The village is probably best known as the terminus of

the Ravenglass and Eskdale Steam Railway, known locally as the La'al Ratty. It was built in 1875 to carry iron ore from the Eskdale valley to the coast. It is now a tourist attraction, popular with children and excited granddads alike. I've ridden its little chuffers several times, but not today, as it's closed.

It's raining lightly in Ravenglass. The village is deserted and slightly eerie, in that brilliant horror movie way. I contemplate going in the pub, but peering through the window for a few minutes – like someone from that aforementioned horror movie – it seems to be open but is completely empty, so I decide against it and return to Eagle One to get warm.

I always enjoy the evenings in my van. With the curtains closed and the heater on, it's cosy and comfortable: my home from home. I generally type up my notes, which are either jotted in a pad, or more usually recorded on a Dictaphone. I make a rough plan of where I aim to go the next day and might perhaps do a small amount of research, if there's a signal and I can get on the internet; I don't research too much though, as I want to discover a place for myself and see what's there when I arrive.

After I've had my tea – a large proportion of which is salad at the moment; one isn't as slim as one used to be – I generally relax and watch a DVD on my laptop. I'm not really a film person, I prefer classic TV, adventure series from yesteryear and comedies.

Each night I have to make the bed up, which is a bit of a faff. I'd love a van with a bed space over the driver's cab, but I've only ever wanted a small van that can go down narrow lanes to clifftops and so on, without getting wedged between hedges. In theory, I *do* have an upstairs bedding area, but it's very small, too small for anyone other than a newborn baby – and it would be like putting the infant on the luggage rack on a train and that's almost universally frowned upon.

The main bed, when fully made up, is very comfortable, but not very large; you couldn't accommodate two people without you both being fully lubricated. I enjoy lying there at night, corner to corner, bathed in the green glow from the fridge light, listening to the wind and the rain and the thrashing of the trees, as I do on this particular night, whilst the Cumbrian elements rage around me.

* * * * * * * * * *

I leave Ravenglass quite early and it's still raining. The road swings constantly and undulates through a very attractive landscape of woodland and green fields. The scenery is now looking more like the picture postcard Lake District. I too am looking more like a postcard of the Lake District – in that I'm quite green. I've been feeling slightly nauseous since I set off on the trip and it seems to be getting steadily worse.

Out at sea, towards the murky horizon, are hundreds of wind turbines; from here they look like the crosses on the graves at a war cemetery. This area has one of the highest concentrations of wind turbines in the world – and no shortage of wind.

Poor Barrow-in-Furness doesn't have a good rep. (I'm not sure the people of Barrow actually *get* The Knowhere

Guide. The local entries are mainly names, people whom the readers presumably don't like: "Ben Williams, Jessica Joel and Michael Arsanay - you know who you are". That's good to know. There is also: "my ex-wife-to-be – she's an ex-whore". I wonder what she does for a living now then. And also the classics: "Drugs", "inbreeding" and "chavs".) If you say "I'm going to Barrow.", which I have done several times recently, the response will usually be something like: "Oh god, *why?*"

In 2008, Barrow was unveiled as the "most working class town" in Britain. It is also an unemployment hotbed; one of the largest of its remaining industries is weapons manufacture. It was once famously a ship building town, constructing warships and later nuclear-powered submarines. Unfortunately for Barrow, the end of the Cold War brought about a reduction of military contracts, which eventually all but finished off the industry. Today, as we've already seen, Barrow is big in renewable energy, with several offshore windfarms. You could say Barrow has moved from nuclear submarines to *new, clear* energy. You could say it, but I'm not sure why you would.

A road bridge links Barrow with Walney Island, which is a twelve-mile-long strip of land adjacent to the mainland, so narrow in places that during really bad storms, the sea can wash right over it. Walney was created from debris dumped there by retreating glaciers – a case of post-glacial fly tipping.

Immediately over the bridge is the suburban centre of Walney, planned as homes for workers at the shipyards. The north of Walney has nice beaches and acres of static holiday homes. As you drive to the south end, called logically "South End", the houses finish and the road degenerates, becoming a single pitted trackway. The landscape becomes suddenly more barren, scraggy and scrubby. It's flat and there are no trees. It feels very remote. The beaches to the north of the island hold no interest for me, but the eerie wilderness to the south is my sort of place.

I arrive at the South End campsite, mainly populated by static caravans in regimented rows. It has a bar and leisure facilities. Yet again, I pay far more than I really want to pay for facilities that I really don't want to use, then set off on foot to explore. Most of the surrounding area is a nature reserve. Some sort of bird is making a plaintive cry across the marshes. I meet a few people out walking in the vicinity of the campsite, but once further away I don't meet a soul and the place has a feeling of being abandoned.

I find one of several bird hides, a jazzily painted wooden structure, at odds with its surroundings rather than trying to blend in. Actually, to call this a hide is downgrading it; it's light and bright and filled with artwork and more like a nature centre and observation lounge. I sit alone, gazing absently over the sand banks at the wading birds that are just unidentifiable specks. Quite naturally I start to think about life, where I'm going, where I've been, where I want to go, where I don't, and who had invented flip-flops and why... My blinking is getting a lot more laboured and I just can't keep my eyes open. I'm very comfortable, pleasantly warm, slumped forwards, dozing. It's quite blissful, but I very wisely force myself to leave the hide before I fall fully asleep.

I continue towards the tapering, octagonal white tower of Walney Lighthouse. It was built in 1804 and is still in operation. It's quite a stunning building in a stunning setting – and I'd quite happily live in it.

I make my way back to the campsite with very heavy feet. I'm feeling very sick and ill today... I have a shower and return to Eagle One. The wind is strong, coursing across the island with nothing to stop it. I fall asleep with the van rocking from side to side like I'm at sea, which only adds to my sickness...

* * * * * * * * * *

I awake and it's Friday. Probably. I *think* it's a Friday. Still tired. Still ill. Sweating, full of anxiety and stress. Nauseous. Everything feels wrong. Everything is a struggle. I pack up. Slowly. And drive off. Slowly. Weaving back through the industrial bowels of Barrow. Slowly.

I stop for fuel; the lady on the till is lovely and chatty and friendly. It immediately perks me up, because if she can be cheerful with her view of Barrow's corrugated roofs and reinforced concrete, then anyone can, could and should. I drive off as happy as a pig in... sick... I start to feel very sick again... very soon... very bad. Really sick. Gut-wrenchingly sick. The nausea is completely taking over. I realise I've felt sick all week, but I've been putting on a brave face and trying to forget about it.

I had been planning to take the ferry across to Piel Island – it was one of the scheduled highlights I was really looking forward to, but the thought of water: choppy, surging, swelling tides, a lurching boat... Oh god... I drive straight past. I arrive at the gates of Conishead Priory on the outskirts of Ulverston, an area I know quite well. I pull into the Priory. I pull on the handbrake and jump out. (It has a café!)

The house is a huge and imposing Gothic pile. The architecture is striking. Again, it would be a great location for a horror movie. After a varied history, like so many great houses it eventually fell into a state of dereliction and was scheduled for demolition. Thankfully, in the mid-Seventies the building was bought by a Buddhist community, who have lovingly renovated it from a state of collapse to a state of karmic glory.

I think I could quite easily become a Buddhist monk. There is far too much materialism in the world and too much corruption. I would very much like to live a simple life. Buddhism is a philosophy rather than a religion; there is no god, just an outline of how to live your life well, and that really appeals to me. I've done a few Buddhism courses in my time, but ironically, I found them to be rather materialistic and they didn't sit right with me.

Because I'm still feeling sick, I decide – like you do – that obviously a coffee and cake might help. I thought that putting something in my stomach would settle it. The café is bright, essentially a conservatory, looking out over an ornamental lawn. At one point, a piercing electronic fire alarm goes off – probably a joss stick related incident – but very swiftly, normal, serene service is resumed.

I have a coffee – bad move – and a "malted flapjack" – worse move. Both are horrible, but I think it's me. The

Priory – on this occasion – isn't delivering the calm and wellbeing I had hoped it would. The coffee and cake really isn't helping my ever-present nausea at all. I continue into Ulverston. ("The stink from Glaxo Wellcome factory", "No High Cultural stuff", "Over milking of the "Stan Laurel was born here" thing".)

It's pouring down, I feel very ill and am getting piss wet through and pissed off, so I call into a lovely little vegetarian café. I opt for a vegetable hotpot from the specials board, thinking something savoury, solid and healthy will help. It doesn't. Again, I think it's me, rather than the food. I go for a slow walk around the town in the rain. Ulverston is very pleasant – not a twee tourist town by any means, but a nice, practical market town with narrow streets and some interesting charity shops. It's famously the birthplace of Arthur Stanley Jefferson, who went on to become Stan Laurel, half of the world-famous double act, Laurel and Hardy. He was originally Charlie Chaplin's understudy. From 1928 onwards, he had moved to America, met Oliver Hardy and they formed their inseparable double act, which only ended when Hardy died in 1957. Laurel officially retired at that point and died in 1965.

My plan was to go for a walk in the surrounding fells, but the gut-twisting nausea is getting worse. I lurch back to Eagle One and abandon Ulverston, as I'd abandoned the Priory, as I'd abandoned Piel Island, thinking that perhaps being focused on driving might take my mind off the sickness, but once behind the wheel, I feel even sicker.

I drive through the rain for several miles along a dual carriageway. The driving really isn't helping, after all.

It isn't helping one bit. *Nothing* is helping. My mouth is running with saliva. I'm drenched with sweat. My stomach is burning. I suddenly feel the unmistakeable internal lurching... There is a layby ahead, so I pull in, slam on the brakes and am suddenly and violently sick into a (thankfully pre-prepared) carrier bag. Eight times. It isn't just being sick, it's like being turned inside out. It's horrible.

I can't believe how long it goes on for. I also can't believe I'm seeing my expensive hot pot again, pooled in the bottom of a carrier bag. When eventually it stops, I just kneel on the floor with my eyes closed. My clothes are sticking to me, like someone has thrown a bucket of water over me. I feel weak and physically exhausted. My stomach feels like I've been punched repeatedly. I collapse onto the settee, unable to remain upright and fall asleep instantly.

* * * * * * * * * *

The world always seems a better place after a good night's sleep. It's a dull, grey morning, but for the first time in days the almost permanent sickness has left my stomach and I feel purged. It's only a short drive to the Cartmel peninsula, but it doesn't stop a huge lorry nearly crashing into me on the dual carriageway; he just pulls out towards me without looking. But then he horns me! *He* horns *me*! He *horns* me! A collision is narrowly avoided and I would have liked to take something positive from this experience, such as *enjoy the moment because it could be your last.* (Actually, that's not all that positive, but I can't see any very positive positives.) The only thing that keeps running through my head is: *he horned me!* And he did, the cheeky bastard! He horned me!

I drive – fuming and obsessing – to the furthest point on the peninsula, to the tiny village of Ravenstown, which is dark and rather severe in the poor light and beneath the low rainclouds. It was originally built to house workers at the nearby airship station.

In comparison, neighbouring Flookburgh seems huge and bustling, hip and swinging. Comparatively. Mainly because it has more than one pub and boasts a market square. It also seems whiter and brighter, which is ironic because it has an unfortunate history; it was ravaged by plague in the 17th Century, then virtually destroyed by fire. On a lighter but more calorific note, on the outskirts of the village is the factory where locally devised, but nationally popular, Sticky Toffee Pudding is made. (No wonder it seems such a happy place.)

A network of single-track leafy lanes lead from the village ever-further from civilisation, ending at a tidal beach at the foot of Humphrey Head. In geographical terms, this is a limestone cliff, the tallest in Cumbria. In historical terms, it has the ludicrous distinction of supposedly being where the last wolf in England was killed. It is the highest point in the area and feels remote and isolated. The holy well here is renowned for its healing properties. I wish I'd had a swig yesterday.

I park in the small, empty car park and begin the climb to the top of Humphrey Head. The path rises steeply over smooth-worn limestone, which seems to be made out of slippery glass. It is a sheer climb in places and quite treacherous. On the summit, it's cold and blowing a gale. Wind-ravaged hawthorn bushes are all completely leafless but festooned with blood-red berries, all their branches bent in the same direction from decades of strong winds. There are sections of exposed limestone pavement and flattened grass. There are views for miles across the flat expanse of Morecambe Bay to the trees of Silverdale. There is a gigantic square structure towards the horizon, far larger than anything else in sight, a huge blot on the landscape and it draws my eye. It's unavoidable. I can't imagine what could be so colossal. (I checked the map later, it is Heysham power station.)

There are some birds, heard but not seen. I don't know what they are, but they're making bird noises, so it seems a pretty good guess. I descend a shallow path towards the beach and walk beneath a sheer cliff face, back towards the car park. An inappropriately jaunty rhyming couplet on a memorial plaque at the base of the rocks reads:

> *"Beware how you these rocks ascend,*
> *Here William Pedder met his end."*
>
> *August 22nd 1857. Aged 10 years.*

This is a nature reserve, but all I spot is a small, dead crab, lying on its back. The River Leven winds across the sand and marshes towards the sea. I have to cross its flow twice, wading through shallower sections, very wary of quicksand for which these parts are renowned, but I make it back to Eagle One unscathed and drive on to the ancient village of Cartmel, famous for its beautiful and distinctive 12th Century Priory. Because the priory served as the local church, it survived Henry VIII's Dissolution of the Monasteries: he had big issues with religious buildings and wives... and chopped both on a regular basis.

The winding streets that lead off from the market square are lined with the most elegant cottages with quite exquisite features, porches, pediments and nice knockers. Cartmel is almost a show village, compared to the other villages I've encountered this morning, which are sturdy and practical, built to withstand the weather over the centuries. And they have done.

* * * * * * * * * * *

Another short drive to Grange-over-Sands, a nice Victorian and Edwardian seaside resort. I follow a path signed for the promenade, a fine, wide, curving walkway with occasional steps leading down to where the sea should be, but there is just a carpet of reeds and rushes: Grange now has no sea. It's sea-free. It has a prom, but the sea has gone. The tides changed and Grange-over-Sands was left high and dry. It's very nice anyway with views across the wide estuary.

As I stroll along, I pass a lady in a very long raincoat with a sleek greyhound. She is talking to the dog in some detail about the weather forecast. Perhaps worryingly, I'm fairly sure I hear the greyhound answering back.

A short way along the prom is the old Lido: boarded up, graffitied, abandoned, collapsing and decaying. There are gaps in the hoarding and I can see the stagnant rainwater filling the peeling pool. Buddleia and willow herb have forced their way up between the cracked paving. It's a sorry sight: a type of amusement now redundant and forgotten. On the hoarding there are pictures as it was in its heyday, when the summers were long and sunny and people enjoyed a simpler life, when a day in the sunshine beside a swimming pool was a memorable day. It's very sad really. I once went to an outdoor pool with a group of friends. We stayed all day messing about in the water – it was a strange and fun day, which felt like something from a film. When I think about it now, it automatically slips into slow motion. All I can remember is the laughter; there was a lot. We never repeated that golden day, and I don't think it *could* have been repeated. Besides, the pool closed down shortly afterwards.

Morecambe Bay is notoriously dangerous. A tractor-like vehicle is stationed at Grange, which goes out to rescue people stranded on the sands, cut off by the rapidly incoming tide. Famously, in 2004, at least 21 Chinese illegal immigrants were drowned while picking cockles. They had been imported – like cargo – into Liverpool via shipping containers and were hired out through local Triads. The emergency services were called, via a mobile phone, but only one person was rescued alive.

I'm bursting – I no longer have a cast iron bladder. (I'm not sure I ever did.) The only toilet I can find is one of those unisex cubicles that charges twenty pence. I generally begrudge paying to have a wee, when I'm spending money to visit a place, but I'm desperate. For your twenty pence, you get an electronically timed fifteen minutes of toiletry solitude, after which the door will unceremoniously open, whether you're ready or not. I use less than two minutes, so I feel a bit short changed. I wash my hands ludicrously slowly to try and get my money's worth.

I walk back through the town itself, which is somewhat disappointing. There's nothing, as such, *wrong* with "inland" Grange, but it seems to consist of several streets of shops filled with people shopping, a main road and parked cars – and I can see all that any day of the week.

I drive away from Grange and at some point, unbeknown to me, I cross my first county border and leave Cumbria behind.

* * * * * * * * * *

If Brendan was with me…

Because this volume is a prequel to *underdogs*, it is by default part of that series. In a way. This trip is undeniably a part of the same voyage, the same circumnavigation of Britain that my dog, Brendan, later joined me on, so it's inevitable that I can't help comparing this solo trip to our joint trips later on. When I began on this journey, I was very happily dog-free. I didn't want a dog; I found the idea of having a dog very restricting. Think of all the things you can't do when you've got a dog! He would probably have found this first leg of the trip tolerable, though the weather would have annoyed him, as would getting out of the van. My funny, quirky, high-maintenance Brendan. Just writing this makes me miss him… even though he's sitting right next to me.

ABOVE: Me, my boy, my van. What a team! (But this is in the future! We haven't met yet.)

ABOVE: The Solway Firth.

CHAPTER 2: THE
LIGHTS FANTASTIC

In which I visit the seaside – several times. I go up Blackpool Tower and am *not* sick into a carrier bag. So, things are looking up!

I park up in Silverdale – a bit confused because it's neither silver nor a dale. I remain behind the wheel for some time, watching in fascination as an elderly lady executes a twenty-seven-point turn. Once she's achieved her goal, she judders off down the street, clutching the steering wheel as though her life depends on it. Which actually it does.

Silverdale is in Lancashire – just – and is part of an Area of Outstanding Natural Beauty. It's certainly beautiful, set in heavy woodland, gently undulating with many attractive dwellings, yet it feels to me like a place where people *live*, rather than a place that welcomes visitors. Charlotte Bronte stayed here as a child and a while later, comedian Victoria Wood lived in the area.

I walk down to the beach, where a young couple are sitting huddled on a bench smoking, trying to keep warm in the bitter wind. Moments like this seem so special, when you're young. It's the kind of thing that would make a cherished memory. Not that they'll probably still be together in years to come. (I'm very cynical.)

The sun might well have his hat on, but it's probably a balaclava. It's gone as suddenly as it had arrived; it looks like rain is imminent. The horizon is hazy and unclear. The sea is at the furthest point out and there are just miles and miles of flat, sandy bay.

I scramble over limestone outcrops, past warnings of the incoming tides and of quicksand. It isn't the most attractive beach; it's just soft mud in places, yet Victoria Wood chose this stretch of coast as her favourite walk. [1]

Victoria Wood was a BAFTA-winning comedian and writer and was awarded a CBE. Much of her humour was observational and she satirically and joyfully embraced the dullness of being British. "Sex is going out of fashion. It's a little trend I started." Sometimes she employed a sardonic or deadpan delivery; sometimes she came across as joyfully naïve; she *always* came across as funny, commenting on the everyday minutiae of life, to which we can all easily relate. Sadly, she died of cancer in 2016.

And this – the beach, the cliffs and the bay – was her favourite walk. Once the limestone ends, the beach is composed completely of sand and mud, sometimes firmly impacted, like rock, but on the next step my foot sinks down eight or ten inches. I can clearly see how hazardous this sort of terrain can be.

Big black birds take off over the sand flats and fade into the dark grey sky. It's only 4pm but the light is failing and the air feels electric and ominous. The walk isn't far on the map, but it takes ages: clambering over seaweed-covered rocks, slipping and sliding, wading through mud. It feels like I'm running on the spot. It starts to get very cold and the only sounds are the lonely calls of the unseen estuary birds and the wind. I feel very far away and very alone. I walk for so long around a seemingly never-ending headland with a cliff rising up at my side. It's quite eerie and I feel very isolated. I haven't seen another person for days... or at least forty minutes. I'm growing very tired of the constant wading through mud and tentatively placing my weight on one foot to test the sand before I step forward. I stop for a rest and sit on a rock. The wind blows, the birds call, the sea trickles ever-nearer with constant menace. Then I hear the welcome rasping of car tyres over a cattle grid, somewhere close by. It's such a comforting noise, because it signifies civilisation, tarmac, a road, freedom! I leap up and find a way up the cliff, climbing over a wall, jumping down, my boots thudding onto the firm, reassuring rain-wet tarmac.

I walk slowly back towards Silverdale. The road is amongst trees at first, but gradually the houses along it increase, until I'm in the heart of the village. I pass Lindeth Tower – it's a tower – an early-Victorian folly: three storeys of castellated stone. Victorian writer, Elizabeth Gaskell, stayed here in the mid-1800s.

I don't particularly enjoy Silverdale. It seems a little like a very nice art gallery, which isn't open to the public. I don't feel it's *un*welcoming, but I don't feel it's all that welcoming either. This is perhaps because I'm feeling quite poignant, thinking about Victoria Wood. There is a campsite in the village where I had planned to stay, but I drive past it, feeling strangely oppressed. I decide I want to be gone.

Listening to The Jam, I continue south along the coast to Bolton-le-Sands, which is famous for... well, nothing really. I don't mean to be detrimental, because it's a nice enough place. It was originally the village of Bolton – just Bolton, plain and simple Bolton; it had no "le" and no "sands". When the railway came, Bolton – the Lancashire slash Greater Manchester town – was on the same line, so they became -le-Sands and -le-Moors respectively.

My new chosen campsite is at the dead end of a dead-end road alongside Morecambe Bay. I am the only person on the site, in an otherwise empty, waterlogged field of vacant pitches. As the evening descends, it starts to feel quite remote. I don't see a living soul. Thankfully, I don't see any dead souls either, but in the midnight hour, the shrieking wind does its best to make me believe that they're there, lumbering.

* * * * * * * * * * *

The living dead didn't get me in the small hours, so with the sun up – not that you'd really know – and the undead banished to the shadows, I drive into Morecambe ("Crime in the resort is getting worser and worser", [As is grammar by the look of it!], "The chances of getting an STD are 100%", "It is chav central"). I park on the seafront at 10am. The brown sea is fully in and breaking over the rock sea defences, sending up tall columns of spray. It's blustery and pouring down. The only people daring to brave the conditions are the hardy souls walking their dogs or the irrepressible elderly, who've lived through a war, so a bit of wind and rain – even when life threatening – isn't going to deter them from a stroll along the prom or a trip down Memory Lane for no reason, other than to get in the way of people rushing to work. The bins along the prom all have their purple plastic bags hauled out by the wind, but they remain attached, flapping like windsocks.

Despite the bad weather and the low grey clouds, Morecambe feels clean and genteel. It was a thriving seaside resort in the mid-20th Century, attracting visitors from Yorkshire because of its railway connections, earning the town its nickname of "Bradford On Sea". Until 1989, it was the venue for the *Miss Great Britain* beauty contest. Flying in the face of current emancipated thinking, the *Miss Morecambe* competition was revived in 2006 to objectify and sexualise women. Or at least the sexy ones. With that in mind, I pass a sign pointing to "Bare Village" and wonder if it's a nudist area. Surely not. If anyone's nudifying today there won't be much to ogle. (I later discover Bare is the name of a locale, and everyone there is fully trousered and topped.)

Two small, white, Scene of Crime police vans keep buzzing past. They drive with some urgency along the promenade – through the pedestrian-only zones – as though there's been a murder, but I can't see any cordoned-off area with police tape flapping in the wind. (Remember: "Crime… is getting worser and worser". No truer words have been speaked.)

I walk along to the aptly named Stone Jetty: it's a jetty and it's made of stone. It was built to carry a railway line, so goods trains could get closer to the ships with their cargoes. It juts out into a treacherous, heaving, boiling sea. The old station at the end is now a cafe. The sign says it should be open, but it isn't, though there is a light on inside and a car outside. As I round the corner of the station building, I spot a smashed window and – putting something and something together and making five – I cleverly deduce that there's been a break-in or at least some vandalism, possibly hence the SOCO police vans? (Definitely "worser and worser".)

Apart from the Stone Jetty, Morecambe today is a Pier-free zone. It carelessly lost two: one damaged by fire in the Flapping 'Thirties and one partially washed away by a storm in the Flared 'Seventies. In the Nondescript 'Nineties, *The World of Crinkley Bottom* attraction came to Morecambe and thrilled literally dozens of people, until it closed thirteen dismal weeks later. Other attraction-closures swiftly followed.

Facing the Stone Jetty is the smooth, oceanic, white, curving form of the famous Midland Hotel. It was built in the 'Thirties as a railway hotel, known as "the great white hope", which is uncannily accurate, in that it's great and white. Architecturally, it is a *Streamline Moderne* building; which – to you and me – means Art Deco. After many years of neglect, it was refurbished and reopened for business again in 2008. With the sea sending spray across the jetty and a sudden squall of rain hammering down, I run to seek solace in the Rotunda café bar of the Midland Hotel. It's so nice to sit in the warmth of this historic building and look out at the battling elements. It's £3.50 for a very small coffee – I don't think I've ever paid that much in my life – but it's nice to have an ocean view.

By the time I've finished my coffee – (I really milk it. The experience, not the coffee; I have that black, as you're supposed to.) – the rain has abated slightly, so I carry on meandering along the prom.

I find myself in a strange town; a town of contradictions. There are some very attractive buildings along Morecambe's seafront. Unfortunately, there are also some rather dated and jaded shops within them. Many of the cafes look very old fashioned – and I don't mean "retro" or "vintage", I mean "out of date and in need of a make-over". Several shops are just plain *odd*. One specialises in bras, but all the ones in the window seem to be huge and gaudy, like only a drag artiste might wear. It all seems so 'Seventies and tired. There's a difference between something being either "of another age" (such as the Midland Hotel) and something being "past it". Make it *traditional*, make it speak of the English seaside, make it indicative of holidays and fun and sunshine, but don't let it become lacklustre and tired.

Further along the front, is a café called *Lubin's*, which is currently closed. This allegedly provided the inspiration for one of Victoria Wood's most memorable and celebrated comedy sketches, where an aged and incompetent waitress, played by Julie Walters, serves "Two soups!" to an impatient couple. I'm not sure this is necessarily something *Lubin's* should be proud of.

On New Year's Day 2011, Victoria appeared in a BBC drama *Eric and Ernie* as Eric Morecambe's mother, Sadie Bartholomew. Eric's real surname was considered a hinderance, so he adopted the name of his hometown. Today the town pays tribute to its most famous son and much-loved entertainer with a bronze, slightly larger than life-sized statue of Eric. It was created by sculptor Graham Ibbeson and unveiled by the Queen in 1999.#2 It quickly became one of the town's most famous landmarks. Despite the rain, the statue captures the likeness of Eric in a joyful pose, one arm up, one arm down, emulating the dance at the end of *The Morecambe and Wise Show*, when the duo sang "Bring Me Sunshine" prior to exiting the stage. The words to the song that became their theme tune are etched into the steps leading to Eric's likeness. They are happy, uplifting words. "Bring me fun. Bring me sunshine. Bring me love." It is undoubtedly true that "in this world where we live there should be more happiness." But there generally isn't. #3

* * * * * * * * * * *

Heysham is a ferry port and also the site of two nuclear power stations: one of which is the huge square structure I have been able to see on the horizon for days.

Old Heysham has a few very nice streets of pretty, whitewashed stone cottages. A leafy footpath leads past the modern church of Saint Peter's – *modern* in that the oldest parts are *only* from the 1300s. The path leads to Heysham Head, an exposed promontory, where the ruins of the ancient St. Patrick's Chapel stand in splendid isolation. And rain. Lots of rain. It really is a wonderful setting, on a clifftop, seemingly cut off from the rest of the world and in another time. It is an atmospheric spot overlooking the sea, with mysterious arches, steps and passages around the rocks. It feels very old and eerie. Probably because it is; at the very least half as old as human history. The remaining walls are remarkably intact and the arched doorway is perfectly preserved.

Of even greater interest are the stone graves: coffin-shaped holes carved into the bedrock close to the chapel. Each would once have contained a body, then had a stone slab or wooden panel placed over the top. The empty hollows are filled with rain water, reflecting the sky and looking otherworldly. It's very windy and difficult to stand. Rain is being thrown down like stones; it's ideal weather for this mysterious location. On a fine day, I could stay here for hours, soaking up the atmosphere and gazing out to sea. But it's not a fine day, so I don't.

It's only a short, but busy drive into the city of Lancaster ("Hostility towards outsiders by stuck up lancastrians" (sic), "The city is always trying to be things its not" (sic), "Theyre all snooty bastards" (sic).) Lancaster is situated on the River Lune; a fine, historic city, known as the Northern City of Ale, due to the number of pubs serving cask ale and the number of northerners drinking it.

I have tea and cake in a quirky vegetarian café. It's cake *plural* – raspberry Bakewell tart. Twice.

Lancaster has many fine examples of Georgian architecture; it is another very handsome town. I have a slow wander around the streets and find that despite all the attractive buildings, Lancaster seems to be largely filled with exactly the same shops you would find on any high street in any town anywhere. This is the modern world.

I'm feeling a bit sluggish after the cake plural and decide a walk might revive me. I decide to try and find Williamson

Park, a Victorian landscaped pleasure ground in the city, created by the First Baron Ashton, millionaire James Williamson. Crowning this ornamental parkland is the Ashton Memorial, built in the early 1900s, in memory of his second wife. It is a commanding Baroque structure which dominates the landscape for miles around, like a gigantic, perfectly-iced wedding cake. Apparently, it stands close to the mathematical centre of the UK. I have seen this impressive domed monument so many times when passing by on the Lancastrian section of the M6, but I've never visited it before. Standing here now I have an overwhelming sense of achievement. I shouldn't do: I didn't build it.

Walking back downhill into the town, I find I have mis-timed things and the schools are turning out. Uniformed kids flood the pavements and I'm engulfed in the crowd. I have to say, they are very well-behaved kids. I spot two lots of graffiti, each quite perplexing and philosophical: THE EARTH IS FLAT on a bench – and MEDICATED in manly pink letters on a wall. They are probably not at all thought-provoking and are references to songs, because in my experience graffiti-ists are not usually philosophers or poets.

I slip out of Lancaster before the hardcore rush hour starts. I find a campsite in Cockerham and after a day of on and off rain, sometimes quite vicious, the *proper* rain sets in for the evening and it means business. This suits me fine, because it's a good excuse to stay in Eagle One and focus on eating and relaxing, which I do to the best of my abilities, with the curtains drawn, the heater on and rain thrumming constantly on the roof.

* * * * * * * * * * *

Morning shows up, bright-eyed and bushy tailed. After the heavy rain in the night, it's a surprise when the grey nothingness of dusk eventually evolves into a beautiful sunny day. I navigate a series of angular single-track lanes across wide, open farmland and park up in a dirt layby on the banks of the Lune Estuary. I walk through the bitter cold and harsh winds along the top of the sea wall that protects grassy fields. A herd of Friesians stand idly around in the mud, chewing lazily and watching me with mild interest.

Out in the swelling waves, Plover Scar Lighthouse comes into view. It's a really attractive little lighthouse, with something of a fairytale feel to it; it looks like a child's drawing or a folly, with lovely Victorian embellishments, such as the weathervane topping the roof. As I understand it, the purpose of a lighthouse is to guide ships, so how – in 2016 – did a ship end up crashing into the beacon itself? The damage was so bad that it was nearly the end for Plover Scar, but thanks to an outcry, this joyful little tower was rebuilt stone by stone and restored to its former glory.

I head back to Eagle One through the wind and the sunshine. I pass an old man on the lane, who is walking painfully slowly, carrying a huge torch in broad daylight, perhaps as a weapon or – judging by the speed he's travelling – maybe he isn't expecting to reach home before nightfall.

I sit in my van with a cup of tea, scanning news articles

on the area. There is growing concern about several bodies being found on the various beaches in the vicinity, believed to be suicides. I used to be a Samaritan, taking calls from potentially suicidal people. The Samaritans remit was to listen and not judge – and not give advice. It was very difficult if a caller had taken an overdose and just wanted someone to talk to, to be with, so they weren't alone when they died. I had one such call, a young woman whose husband and young child had been killed in a road accident several months earlier and she had suffered and struggled for so long, but it had all been too much; she had given up and taken an overdose. She was weak and dizzy and was finding it difficult to speak and to stay awake. I repeatedly asked her if she would like me to call an ambulance, but she refused. There was no facility to see or trace the number. In the end she said she could no longer hold the phone. She thanked me groggily and hung up. I never found out what had happened to her.

A single lady pulls into the parking space next to me. For a few minutes, she sits staring out at the estuary. She seems sad, reflective, poignant. She looks like someone who might be considering suicide… I feel agitated, awkward, impotent. I'm still deliberating my course of action when she suddenly lunges at a tin foil parcel of sandwiches and begins eating her lunch with fevered enthusiasm. So, I eat mine.

* * * * * * * * * * *

I arrive in Lytham and check into an "Adults only" camp site, which is much less X-rated than it might sound. The reception smells like a dentist. I mention this to the woman manning the desk. "Someone else said that…"

She frowns. "I think it must be these lilies." There is a huge arrangement of flowers in a gigantic vase, the type you might find at the reception of a very corporate office block, but not on a campsite. They look strangely out of place.

The site is clean and tidy, but not exceptional. It's perfectly adequate; it has all mod cons, but is rather functional for the seriously inflated prices they're charging. I'm really not sure how campsites get away with it. It strikes me that running a campsite might be an ideal job for me. But I'd end up keeping the gates locked and not allowing people in. So, perhaps not.

According to my research, Blackpool is one of the worst places to live and has a very high drugs problem. They tend to gloss over that in the brochures. (Blackpool: "the beach the people the buildings the sky the ground the everything" (sic), "scumbags and deadbeats", "The place is full of druggies, alcoholics, chavs, self-important gays, kebab owners".)

I haven't mentioned SatNav Sally yet, though she has been my constant, infuriating and ineffectual companion since I left home. She was a hand-me-down from Nicky's dad – an ex-copper. He handed her down – a little too enthusiastically, I thought – saying she was "a bit out of date", but she was "better than nothing". He was quite wrong about that: *nothing* is generally a more reliable option than SatNav Sally. (His name, not ours.) He also neglected to mention her really *bad attitude* and her impatience. She tells me to turn left immediately, which would mean me driving into the sea. She repeats it: "Turn left and drive straight ahead." So, across the beach and into the sea? Perhaps that explains the bodies on the beach – people obeying their SatNavs. I ignore her. You may be wondering why I even bothered to plug her in… because I'm wondering that too. I unplug her again and follow my instincts… and keep the sea on my left, without actually entering it at any point.

I cut through Saint Anne's, which is one of the increasing number of places whose name seems to have (usually) lost its apostrophe. But not here, my friend, not here. It seems genteel, affluent and attractive. It has very wide streets and everyone perambulating along those wide streets looks happy. It seems clean and organised: a very suburban and middle-class seaside destination. Perhaps too perfect: the Stepford of seaside resorts. Maybe it's something in the air, because I'm feeling contented and relaxed just briefly passing through it.

However, the moment I cross into Blackpool it all instantly changes. There is an area of wasteland between the two towns, soon to be built on I would imagine; this serves as a no-man's-land between the two destinations, it marks the border. The change is immediate and undeniable. Everything is suddenly tacky, scruffy and rough. I park down a back street, but I'm worried about leaving Eagle One here. Most of the shops are closed and have metal shutters pulled down. It feels dejected, rejected, depressed and depressing.

Yet Blackpool has many iconic features. The Tower is iconic. The *three* piers are iconic. The trams *were* iconic, but have been replaced by functional and characterless modern versions, which provide a very good service, but have no character. Blackpool is synonymous with the seaside, the somewhat low-brow seaside admittedly, but it's famous, it's on the world map. Where Morecambe has a smattering of the tacky seaside about it, Blackpool goes full throttle. It has embraced tat and made it its own.

I walk along the wide prom towards the Tower, which fills me with excitement. It dominates the seafront; it dominates everything for miles around. The lattice structure and the tapering shape strongly resemble the Eiffel Tower, but it's here, in front of me, in Blackpool, not in Paris. There are a few people walking along, mainly couples arm in arm for support against the wind. They have their hoods up and their hands in their pockets and are hunched forward in the cold. And yet it's sunny again. Moments later a rainbow appears, spanning the sky over Blackpool and ending at the Tower itself. It has to be an omen. Or a rogue banner left over from a Pride celebration.

Two Victorian, Lancashire architects, James Maxwell and Charles Tuke, designed the Tower. Tragically, by the time it opened, only three years later in 1894, they had both died. It has a very forward-thinking design, so it apparently (and disconcertingly) sways gently in heavy winds. The Tower wasn't painted properly during its first three decades and became corroded, leading to talk about demolishing it – mirroring the fate of another tower further along the coast at New Brighton. However, thankfully it was decided to rebuild it instead. In the early 'Twenties all the steel was painstakingly replaced, piece by piece.

The Tower is usually painted a dark red. Today, despite the wind, there appear to be men – or *people* rather –

in hi-viz clothing suspended by ropes. Presumably, like the Forth Bridge, the painting is an on-going, cyclical job. The top of the Tower was painted silver in 1977 for the Queen's Jubilee and gold in 1994 to mark its own centenary.

I've wanted to go up the Tower for years, so I go and buy a ticket, which turns out to be very confusing, because there are countless deals on all of Blackpool's many attractions, various offers, packages and bundles, doubling up, doubling down, pass Go and collect two hundred pounds. Do I want to go in the dungeon as well? Or the waxworks? Or the ballroom? Or Banana World? Or Mobility Plus? Or Somewhere Else? No, I don't. I *just* want the Tower. Purely and simply the Tower. I don't want my photograph taking at the top and putting on a T-shirt or a mug or a pencil sharpener. I want to go up this historic landmark, as generations before me have done. I want to have a look round, enjoy the experience and then come down again – the slow way, via the lift.

It's all very stressful. In the end, I get my plain, simple, adult single vanilla ticket… which costs a pound more than advertised on their website. I could complain… I *should* complain, but I can't face all the laborious explanations and small print, the clauses and excuses, so I let it go. (But I still mourn that pound.)

There is a half hour wait for the next lift, so I go to the café to get a coffee, but the café is already closed. It's 4.05 in the afternoon and the Tower, Ballroom and other attractions are still open, but the café is closed, even though there are a growing number of people waiting idly for the 4.30 lift up the Tower. They would possibly all have bought drinks... and most likely chips. I sit at a table anyway, minus coffee, looking out of the window at the sea, the beach and the prom. I like what Blackpool used to be and what it stood for: old fashioned seaside and low-brow fun. I just don't like what it has become: stag parties and hen nights... and low-brow fun.

A few years ago, I was stopped by a market researcher in Manchester and asked if I would ever consider a holiday in Blackpool. I said no, I barely know you. She persevered, pressing for an answer. I said no and it was an unequivocal no. I said no and I meant it. She told me – a little bit desperately, I thought – that the town had been given a makeover and there were plans to do this and that and probably the other... I said no, it wasn't my kind of place; I liked the countryside, I liked being away from crowds. And yet here I am, holidaying in Blackpool. I nearly bypassed it, but then I changed my mind and I'm not really sure why. But this isn't really a holiday, it's a trip. It has a motive. I've come here to observe the place, in all its deep-fried glory, not be entertained by it.

As I've said, one of the reasons I'm keen to see the Tower, is that it's a historical feature, it's a landmark, people have been coming here for well over a century... Victorians, Edwardians, gents and ladies, flappers and slappers: they came like the clappers. It has stood proudly, steel and iron... swaying gently in the ferocious northern winds. It was iconic. It *is* iconic. It has an awful lot to live up to.

My first disappointment is the compulsory "4D" film. (I've no idea.) I just want to go up the Tower, but everyone has to don a pair of plastic glasses and lean against a railing – there aren't any chairs – then we're subjected to a film of a chaotic, swirling flight around Blackpool itself, which has very little to do with the Tower and focuses on things that can leap out of the screen at you. Several times we get sprayed with foam from the ceiling whilst the floor vibrates. The Victorians, Edwardians, gents and ladies, flappers and slappers didn't get sprayed with foam and vibrated! This is obviously designed as family-friendly fun, but to me it ruins the timeless experience that visitors have enjoyed for over a hundred years, so I swirl my frock-coat and make for the lift at my earliest convenience. The lift isn't very big. A sign says it can carry 32 people or 250 kg. There are less than 32 of us, but judging by the size of some of my companions, we can't be much under the 250kg limit and we're packed in *very* tightly, so tightly I think I might have started a relationship with the woman in front of me. Cad that I am, once we're at the top and the doors open, I'm off and away without another thought for her.

So, I step out into what is currently known as the Blackpool Tower Eye. At 380 feet, it is the highest observation deck in North West England. There are two higher public levels, but they're outside and are closed today due to the high winds.

The whole experience is a bit disappointing really. And also iconic. It's both… at the same time… in different ways. It's disappointingly iconic. There's a bar and there's pop music. There's a view for miles on each side; the only problem is… the view from Blackpool Tower is inevitably of Blackpool… and it isn't the best-looking town. A bird's eye view gives you a look at the roofs, the car parks and the extractor fans, reinforced concrete, bricks and mortar. I can see people walking on the pavements, couples, families, lone people, wheelchairs, pushchairs and dogs. Life from a window. But it's still Blackpool.

In 1998, the so-called "Walk of Faith" was opened at the top of the tower. It is two floor panels made of glass. Very thick glass. (One hopes.) It's very amusing watching people pluck up the courage to step onto it. They are always tentative and grimacing, holding onto a wall or a friend. I confess, I do the same thing – I skirt uncertainly around the edge first before shuffling my way hesitantly towards the centre. Looking down, there is just the pavement below. Even though you know it isn't going to break, your senses won't let you believe that. It's thrilling. And terrifying. But mainly thrilling. I think.

There is a group of Scottish support workers with a party of wheelchair users. One of the staff, a chunky bloke, hurls himself at the glass floor and poses for photographs, mouth open, hands and legs flailing, as though he's falling. It doesn't seem to amuse the service users, but the staff all laugh. He has a great, fun, inclusive attitude and I can't help keeping a professional eye on the group. A year ago, this is the sort of job I would have been doing; support work had been my main profession for a decade and I really miss it.

One of the best things about the vista, is the uninterrupted view of the so-called 'Comedy Carpet' on the prom in front of the Tower, which is an "art installation" by Gordon Young. It was unveiled in 2011 and celebrates the catchphrases of over a thousand comedians. It cost well over two million pounds to install, made up of granite letters set into the ground. All the greats of yesteryear are represented, showmen (and women) who would have played at Blackpool; Les Dawson, Morecambe and Wise, Tommy Cooper, the Two Ronnies, Victoria Wood, right up to the modern breed, with the likes of Jimmy Carr and Peter Kay. Every famous and much-loved comedian is present. And Jim Davidson.

It's quite poignant that the largest letters – and those closest to the Tower – read: "NICE TO SEE YOU, TO SEE YOU NICE" – the well-known catchphrase of Bruce Forsyth, who died earlier in the year.

I buy a bottle of beer – because I can. I drink it gazing out at the sea and then I come down. I feel the Tower is cheapened with its current tacky family fun stylings, but it probably attracts more people than a traditional historical approach would, so it makes good business sense. I'm a bit disappointed, but glad I've at last done it.

I step out into the icy cold air, walk a matter of yards, then turn into the Wetherspoons pub next door, *The Albert and the Lion,* housed in an art deco building complete with corner clock tower. It was formerly a Woolworths (RIP Woolies). It's less impressive inside, noisy and busy, but good natured. I have a pint and a chickpea and spinach curry and make free with their Wi-Fi. I'm not familiar with Stanley Holloway's monologues, but Albert and the Lion is one of the most famous and features a man-eating lion at the Tower Circus, who – without any men to eat – swallows a little boy, Albert, whole, which is liable to play havoc with his diverticulitis, because you're supposed to chew your food. The Tower Circus, while still open, has commendably not had animal acts since 1990.

* * * * * * * * * * *

I have already bemoaned the loss of the traditional trams, which looked so... well, *traditional* as they cruised up and down the Golden Mile. (Sorry to be so Imperial, but "The Golden 1.609 Kilometre" just doesn't work.) The old trams are still in existence – a solitary one passes by – but they are now for private hire only. I want to get to Fleetwood and the most obvious way is via Blackpool's rather characterless but efficient modern tram service. The Scottish carers with the disabled group also board the same tram.

A woman gets on with two dogs – one is a whippet, the other is some tiny thing with its head jutting from the collar of the woman's coat. She sits next to me, but when I smile at the little dog, she gives me a dirty look and quickly changes seats. She might have thought I was beaming at her breasts.

Looking along the tram, virtually everyone is staring down at their phone, apart from the carers. I can hear their chatter and their warm bonhomie from further along the carriage. It makes me quite poignant – it's that time of day again. As the daylight fades on the suburbs of Blackpool through the windows, I find myself in another reflective mood.

I can see the sun starting to set quite unspectacularly over the sea: no colour, no burning sky. Everything looks very suburban on the landward side and I can hear the traffic and other sounds from the street. As we near Fleetwood, the sea is lost and the line travels through solid suburbs, semi-detached houses with gardens paved over as wider driveways, schools and local shops. This is Fleetwood.

("The smell from the fish factory", "the police just dont listen" (sic), "The bloody toursits (sic) who think they own the place", "The people who live there".)

The Scottish party get off in Fleetwood town centre; they all look exhausted after a full day of fun. The tram continues to the end of the line. I am the only person left on board at this point. I step out of the brightly lit interior into a biting cold wind and a rapidly descending darkness. Fleetwood is deserted. Trees and shrubs thrash and telegraph wires whistle. Cars look abandoned, as though it's some post-apocalyptic film. It's very odd and unsettling.

Fleetwood, of course, is the home of the most humorous of lozengers. Who hasn't uttered a line such as: "I was sucking a Fisherman's Friend" causing much hilarity. They have been exported all around the world – possibly solely because of their comedy value.

I visit both of the town's remaining lighthouses, but my visit to Fleetwood is fleeting, as it's too cold to linger longer. I return to the tram – the same tram – and wait for it to begin its return journey. It's now completely dark and as we arrive on the outskirts of Blackpool, it comes as a very pleasant surprise to see the famous Illuminations are up and lit. I haven't been since I was a child, when the whole thing was quite simple and basic, but no less spectacular, because people were impressed by simpler things then. Today, it's all hi-tech, multi-media, computer controlled, flashing, shimmering, lasers, 3-D – probably 4-D – all encompassing, all expenses paid, a wonderland of vibrant colour and light. The highlight (for me) is several levitating Technicolor daleks and a Tardis. It's all quite astounding. It's something from the past brought up to date in a hugely successful way. Go Blackpool!

I alight at the Central Pier, where there's a poster for Madam Tussaud's, but I don't recognise *any* of the "celebrities". They're probably all reality TV "stars" from *Big Brother* or *The Only Way Is Essex*. Looking back towards the Tower, Blackpool looks like Vegas with coloured lights strung along the road and the Tower itself alight. It's magical. But turning from the prom road onto a side street, Blackpool suddenly looks much less magical. All the hotels boast licensed bars and are all garishly lit, many with red lighting, like brothels, but without exception the bars I pass are all completely empty. It all seems very dated now.

I nervously turn the final corner and thankfully see Eagle One is still there and still intact. I get on board and foolishly ask SatNav Sally to return me to the campsite. She directs me in completely the opposite direction, heading back towards Fleetwood. I ignore her and drive through the wide, orange-lit streets of Saint Anne's. She keeps insisting I do a U-turn, which again I ignore. When we arrive in Lytham, I start to listen to her, because I really can't remember where the site is and it all looks so different in the dark. I follow her guidance, duly taking a left here and a right there, then there are no more houses and no more street lamps and the road narrows and it really doesn't look right. There are hedges on either side now and it's become a single-track lane. I don't know how she can have got me somewhere so unpopulated and deserted so quickly. "Continue ahead" she haughtily instructs.

Suddenly, we're running alongside a wire mesh fence. "Turn right now." she says. It's a gateway into a muddy field, rutted and waterlogged. Perhaps the mud has been churned up by the countless vehicles driven by the hapless people who have blindly obeyed their SatNavs. "Turn right!" she insists. I swear at her and continue ahead. Then we pass what looks like a control tower… and a radar… We seem to be on an airfield. The road abruptly ends, blocked off directly before the runway. I have to do a three-point turn. When we pass the open field she starts up again, "Turn left! Turn *left!*" I refuse again and yank her plug from the cigarette lighter. I'm sure she swears at me, but she's low on battery power and I don't fully catch it. I'll have to find the site the old-fashioned way, the *proper* way: I look at the map. We get there without any further problems.

The campsite is fairly quiet and – unlike the front at Blackpool – is still unimpressive at night.

* * * * * * * * * * *

If Brendan was with me…

For a start, I wouldn't have been able to go up the Tower. Even if it was dog-friendly I would never have got Brendan in the lift, though the "Walk of Faith" would have presented no problem for him, as one of the few things he isn't afraid of is heights. He would have wandered out onto the glass, yawned and sat down. Interestingly, the trip up the Tower remains one of the most memorable parts of the trip and I would gladly do it again. I wanted a timeless Victorian experience and got something much more modern and considerably less timeless, but it was still iconic.

I don't think Brendan would have liked Blackpool very much, unless for some reason it was closed for the day and there were no people around. He would have wholeheartedly approved that the expensive campsite didn't allow children, but would probably have started a campaign to have adults banned as well.

NOTES

#1: Many years ago, I was compiling a book, which contained the favourite walks of celebrities. Victoria was one of the celebrities who kindly agreed to take part.

#2. The "late Queen" this would now read, as we have a king on the throne. This was pre-Covid - it was a different world.

#3. This song now has a deeper and more personal significance, as it was the closing song at my dad's funeral, which was held during lockdown when singing wasn't permitted. Like I said, it was a different world.

Above: The Ashton Monument, Lancaster.

Above: Eric Morcambe, Morcambe Bay.

Above: Blackpool Tower.

CHAPTER 3: LANCS, MANCS AND SCOUSERS.

In which I ruminate and visit "Another Place", then have a blow-out on the motorway. The world is due to end... and it doesn't seem at all unlikely.

Another day, another bright, sunny start. I drive into Lytham to have a look round. It has a restored windmill, which I remember from childhood visits, standing on the attractive green. As children, once we saw the windmill it meant we were nearly at our holiday destination, Saint Anne's-on-sea. Lytham also has a YMCA, where you can apparently have a good time and hang out with all the boys.* Lytham also has a wealth of very attractive detached properties – but there isn't a song about them.

---

* This claim is made by the Village People, and expressly not the YMCA plc.

"Lytham St Annes" (sic) has always confused me, but it is apparently a conurbation, a co-joining of the two towns of Lytham and St. Annes-on-the-Sea (sic) to form a single seaside resort. Even somewhere so seemingly affluent has faced cuts in these austere times; the library having been recently closed by the council.

St Anne's-on-the-Sea was a Victorian planned town, hence its wide streets which form a grid pattern. It seems clean, green and attractive – all helped by the sun, of course. Contributors to our old friend, the Knowhere Guide, seem united in their complaints about the town: "the old people!" and that's about it. It certainly appeals to a lot of mature folk, but at the opposite end of the scale there is plenty here to amuse the family. We came several times in my early childhood, when I was in single figures and short pants. We always had a great time, but then that was the pre-digital age. There is perhaps little to appeal to the generations in between the elderly and the very young, who need thrills, excitement, sex, booze, more sex, flashing lights and sex. I'm sure people probably *do* have sex here occasionally, but it doesn't scream "sex" at you… and it probably involves liniment and support bandages, some complaining and a lot of clock-watching.

I walk along to the pier and through an amusement arcade with its cacophony of tunes, flashing, winking and blinking, beeping and bleeping. It is completely deserted. As though to show how out of date it all is, one of the top prizes you can win is a Rubik's Cube. As I'm leaving, I pass the first customer of the day, a wiley chancer in jogging pants, trying to beat the machines. He has a hungry look of desperation and addiction as he feverishly piles coins into the slot with yellowed fingers.

There is a photographic display of the golden years of the resort, with Victorian couples strolling arm in arm, the men in top hats, the women in long dresses and bonnets, carrying parasols. This was a time when the well-to-do folks enjoyed the chance to see and be seen, to go somewhere and perambulate. For the less fortunate, a day at the seaside once a year, breathing clean air and anything other than not being at work in a mill was good enough. We are so spoiled now.

I find a café and have an Americano whilst looking out over the sea. Everyone looks up as a staggering vagrant stumbles in and lurches towards the counter. I expect the manager to eject him, but instead he says a cheery hello. The vagrant goes behind the counter, pulls on a long apron and disappears into the kitchen. He is apparently the chef. I decide I definitely won't be eating here.

I could idle longer at Saint Anne's, enjoying the sunshine and sedentariness, annoying the local youth by not being old, but older than them, but I'm on a mission. Merseyside is calling. I have a tricky moment whilst leaving the area, when – at a busy crossroads – the traffic lights suddenly fail and all the various lanes start going at once. I slide through unscathed and see in my rear-view mirror that all traffic in each direction has stopped dead in a gridlocked mess.

I pass a bearded hitchhiker with a sign reading M6 SOUTH. I'm going via the M6. I'm going South. The trouble is, he looks like a killer. A bearded killer. A bearded, hitchhiking killer. A scruffy man who's reluctant to shave and has only murder and hitchhiking on his mind. In no particular order. He's a daytripper and doesn't have a ticket to ride. And when I regretfully don't stop for him, he glares at me with the look of a bearded killer, as though to prove the point.

I feel guilty, but I have a "no bearded killers" policy, so I slide the Beatles into the CD player and continue my magical mystery tour. With a little help from my friends, I soon forget about him.

* * * * * * * * * * *

Charnock Richard services on the M6, is (not surprisingly, due to its location) full of Lancs, Mancs and Scousers. Sitting there in the car park I have a Scouse "businessman" in the car next door with his window open, conducting his "business deals" in a car park, always at work, eight days a week, doing dodgy deals to outwit the taxman. I don't want to resort to stereotypes, but it does seem that in order to disprove the myth that all Scousers are on the rob, he's overcompensating by having all his "business conversations" via loudspeaker. It's deafening.

I've stopped to have my lunch, not intentionally spy on people – that's just a perk. A bloke wearing a Grangemouth Triathlon top pulls in with a bike and canoe on the roof rack of his car. A triathlon – three forms of severe exercise and between two and three times too many. Unless there's a cake course in between, it's not for me.

I power up Eagle One and we continue along the motorway, passing a massive graffito on a bridge, somewhere on the outskirts of Liverpool: "Pies of financial reset". I've also seen "The Pies The Pies" on the M6. Perplexing. (A Google search later on reveals that the Pies are a legendary Liverpool band... of graffiti-ists and commercially unsuccessful musicians.)

I'm driving into a city overrun with cars. There are roadworks everywhere and diversion signs that lead you away from where you want to be, then abandon you. SatNav Sally is getting hysterical and I'm getting very pissed off.

Down a backstreet in Seaforth, I pass a pub called *The Cock and Seaman*. I do a doubletake because I assume I've misread it... but I haven't. The hanging inn sign shows a bearded, tattooed sailor-type with his arm round a cockerel. An unlikely pairing, but it could have been worse if they'd opted for a more lurid image.

(Another Google search tells me that the pub was formerly the *Doric*, but is under new ownership by a two-man team who own a string of pubs, usually with "cock" in the title. The locals aren't very impressed and many are taking it the wrong way.) [1]

A short drive through Waterloo, where – according to Abba – Napoleon did surrender (Oh yeah!) [2] and I arrive at my destination at last, Crosby Beach. (Crosby: "Too many crap bars", "LITTER", "Old people and 'Care in the Community' releases", "the gangs".)

Liverpool is a sprawling city. Like any sprawling city it has bad bits. Crosby doesn't appear to be one of them, at least it doesn't appear so to a visitor. A range of sandhills separates the pleasant Victorian suburb of painted houses from the beach. The houses are quite stunning with beautiful period detail, pediments, balconies and verandas. Amongst them is the former home of Thomas

Ismay, who owned the White Star Line, who built the ill-fated *Titanic.*

Since 2007, Crosby Beach has been the permanent home of the controversial art installation, *Another Place* by sculptor, Sir Antony Gormley. It consists of cast iron figures of Gormley's own body, which stand at regular intervals over a two-mile stretch of the beach, staring out to sea. They are a dominant presence; it is impossible not to take notice of them. The statues are naked and anatomically correct. I was expecting a smooth, rounded, androgynous crotch area, but no, Sir Antony had gone for full detail. I can now reveal Antony Gormley isn't circumcised. Whoever you are – regardless of gender, sexuality, age, height, hair colour or political persuasion – as you approach the statues, the first thing you notice is – he ain't got no pants on. I watch with some amusement as people make their way to a statue, their eyes look from the face down the body and without fail their gaze comes to rest on the groin area. It's an unavoidable and unconscious natural reaction.

Originally, the statues were due to be relocated in November 2007. Despite opposition from certain quarters, including the Coast Guard and watersports enthusiasts, permission has been granted for the installation to remain on a permanent basis, which has delighted Sir Antony Mark David Gormley, OBE, himself. His other most famous and visual work is the just-as-controversial *Angel of the North* at Gateshead. But that has pants on. Probably.

Some of the iron Gormleys are regularly consumed by the sea and it's eerie to watch them standing stock still as the water steadily rises around them. The ones that get submerged are covered with barnacles and seaweed. They are silent, watchful, poignant, calm, indifferent, uninhibited... and a bit rusty.

As a piece of art, I wonder what they're supposed to *mean*. To me, they make me think of suicidally depressed people walking into the sea. They do look uncannily like corpses in various states of decomposition, flaking and discoloured, stained, covered in barnacles, especially the faces, with the noses and lips corroding away. But conversely, they're looking out over the waves to another place, which suggests optimism. They're a fascinating feature of this beach and have put it on the world map. It's only when you start trying to explain the meaning that they come across as utter bollocks. Two hundred to be exact. On one hundred cast iron statues.

I return to Eagle One and catch a few shreds of news. There has been a mass shooting in America. There is some public hysteria about a so-called Planet X which was foretold to collide with the Earth; NASA has strenuously denied its existence, while simultaneously revealing that a giant asteroid is approaching the Earth. Nostradamus warned "beware of the yellow men" and Korean Kim is gleefully testing nuclear missiles. A man has been convicted of trying to recruit children into ISIS by showing them videos of beheadings. The world is in a mess and I quite enjoy being out of the loop and not feeling very much a part of it.

* * * * * * * * * *

I'm really ticking off the counties now. Yesterday I was

in Cumbria. This morning I was in Lancashire, this afternoon Merseyside and now, strictly speaking, I'm entering Cheshire. I've been here, there and everywhere.

I follow a long and winding road out of Liverpool to the strange village of Hale – only just in Cheshire, but on the borders with Merseyside and – quite literally – at the side of the Mersey itself. The old part of the village is very attractive, it has some picture postcard village scenes, complete with thatched cottages, then a new-build estate, then a council-type estate; it doesn't seem sure what to make of itself – and I'm not too sure either, but the cloying greyness isn't helping. The damp air is smothering everything; the landscape has gone into black and white and looks dismal and threatening.

Hale is famous for being the home of John Middleton (1578–1623), better known as the *Childe of Hale* – for some reason – who was reputed to be nine feet, three inches tall. There's a bronze statue of him, supposedly lifesize, outside the pretty church.

I'm flying through the village and along a dead-end lane, which terminates in a small car park. I continue on foot along a dirt trackway between farmed fields. The scene now looks very un-Cheshire-like. It is suddenly cold and bleak, the fields are bare and sodden; ahead there's a view over the industrialised Mersey-side of the Wirral. At the end of the track stands Hale Head lighthouse, a white tower and a keeper's cottage that looks shabby and in need of a lick of paint. It is sadly redundant as a lighthouse: no light shines from its ample tower and the lenses are housed in the Merseyside Maritime Museum. The accompanying cottage is now a private dwelling. I wonder what it would be like to live in this isolated and eerie spot, on the edge of the tidal Mersey. It's very grey and barren. Although I love lighthouses, I'm not sure I'd like to be here at night.

I scramble down a short sandy cliff to the beach in front of the cottage, which is strewn with washed-up debris, mainly plastic bottles and tin cans. Slabs of sandstone make up most of the beach with initials and names carved into the soft stone. There is also spray-painted graffiti on the sea wall of the lighthouse. It feels very sinister.

I hurry back to Eagle One, running most of the way along the dirt track, because I know this area has a high crime rate for vehicles being broken into. In the car park I spot a police sign I hadn't noticed before, warning of car crime and number plate theft. As I round the van to enter via the sliding side door, my feet crunch in a sea of broken safety glass from countless broken car windows, fortunately, not belonging to Eagle One. If I'd seen this when I arrived, I'd probably not have left my precious van. Regardless of crime stats, I remain in situ while I have my tea.

Some time later, the lighthouse family arrive home in their car; man, woman and children. The father gets out and opens the gate, glancing suspiciously at me for several seconds. Next, a sprightly old geezer with binoculars passes through the car park and stares at me – I can't work out whether it's suspicion or bemusement. He's clearly a tweeter – the estuary is renowned for its birdlife and since it was cleaned up a few years ago, the Mersey is teeming with – of all things – octopuses.

I need somewhere to stay for the night. I do a Google search for sites in the area and book on a site called Halewood Caravan Park. The nice lady on the phone asks how long I'll be. "I'm just in Hale," I say, "So only a few minutes."

I drive from Hale to Halewood. It takes less than five minutes. I find Halewood Caravan Park. It's a Park Homes development with several signs at the gate warning 'No Intruders', 'Strictly Private', 'Keep Out' and so forth, which seems odd. I ignore all these and drive round the circular driveway. It's full of static homes, tightly packed together. There is no space for touring vehicles and no reception of any kind – I have a bad feeling about it. I drive up and down the road a few times in case I've got the wrong place, but it's the only Halewood Caravan Park. I hate admitting defeat, but I phone the site again.

"I'm sorry, but I'm at the gate now and it doesn't look like a campsite."

The lady hesitates. "I can't see you. Where did you come from? Because when you said you were in Hale I didn't know where you meant."

"Hale… Hale village…"

"I've never heard of Hale."

"Hale village? Just down the road from Halewood."

"Nope. Never heard of it."

I feel exasperated. "It's on the Cheshire and Merseyside border."

"Oh… that's not round here."

"I don't understand…"

"We're in Staffordshire."

"But… I found a website… it's got your phone number and the postcode for this place."

"It's a mistake then." she says dismissively. As I'm almost certainly no longer a customer she has suddenly lost all interest and isn't concerned about correcting the mistake on the website.

"Oh… Well, I'm nowhere near Staffordshire, so I'll have to cancel." She hangs up without another word.

I sit for a few minutes, not sure what to do. I recheck the website and sure enough the entry is wrong. I feel suddenly very tired and I've had enough of pissing around with campsites. I drive to a wide layby behind a grass verge and sit watching the already-meagre light fading over the empty fields. With the light gone, I can't keep my eyes open. There are no signs telling me not to stay overnight, besides I'm only sleeping. I lie down fully clothed and fall asleep.

* * * * * * * * * *

Good day sunshine. It's been a hard day's night, but I feel fine. I'm still in Cheshire. Not that it looks or feels much like Cheshire at the moment.

I can't say a lot about Widnes, except it seems to be made up of busy roads, a lot of roadworks, a lot of roundabouts and there is a lot of industry. Every time I've been here it smells of lard. (Apparently, the stench is from animal carcases being burned.) It's always made me retch.

Widnes's other claim to fame – worldwide fame, in fact – is that Paul Simon wrote *Homeward Bound* while waiting for a train at Widnes station and smelling lard. No wonder the song features the lines: "I wish I was... homeward bound." There was once a commemorative plaque at the station – but it kept getting stolen.

The Knowhere Guide has a lot of input about Widnes. One contributor refers to the locals as "Widiots". Top amongst the reasons for hating Widnes are: "the foul smell", "plastic Scousers", "the stench", "the aggression", "the lack of cute guys", "the fat-arsed women", "crackheads and smackheads".

On the plus-side, it's home to the Runcorn-Widnes Bridge, which I have always thought is a marvel of engineering. It's visible for miles around; it's eye-catching and distinctive, an arching lattice framework spanning a narrow point in the River Mersey. It was opened in 1961, but widened in the 'Seventies, when it was rebranded as Jubilee Bridge. It's an amazing feature. Unfortunately, it links Widnes and Runcorn.

I'm surprised to find I'm being funnelled not to the Jubilee Bridge, but to a newly built crossing over the Mersey, called the Mersey Gateway – still between Widnes and Runcorn. I can see the lovely old arched span of the Jubilee Bridge on my right as we glide over the river. The Mersey; it begins in my hometown of Stockport beside the motorway embankment, where two smaller rivers meet. There is very little fuss or celebration. It ends in Liverpool, of course, where it's suitably famous and people write songs about it, Gerry Pacemaker ferries across it and the Beatles are immersed in it, because they apparently all live in a submarine. A yellow one.

The metal supports of the bridge are painted a very odd, pale mint green, which looks like undercoat. Judging by the number of traffic cones around, the bridge still isn't completely finished. It isn't a great experience. It gets you across the river, but it has very little class compared to the old bridge. I reach the Runcorn side; there are no toll booths in sight. I assume they haven't been built yet.

Runcorn is another industrial town, with a New Town tacked onto it. I do a Google search for images and the majority of photographs are of the impressive Jubilee Bridge, plus a few factories thrown in for good measure. And that is essentially Runcorn. One website refers to it as the "slum of the northwest". ("The Knowhere Guide" cites "slags", "gangs" and "the smell drifting over from Widnes"). Let's move on. It's quite a relief to hit the comparatively attractive motorway.

The M56 – it takes the English into Wales – and presumably works the other way round as well. One noticeable feature at this point – apart from all the funnels and chimneys of Frodsham ("bad public transport", "Runcorn scallies who come on holiday to Frodsham and drink too much") and Ellesmere Port ("chavs", "drugs", "parking charges") is the wooded hillside of Helsby ("no police", "the state of the local park", "the blue rinse brigade"), rising up from the Cheshire Plain. From this angle you can see the outline of a face in the sandstone cliff, known locally as the "Old Man of Helsby". My mum always used to tell us to look for it when we had day trips to Chester ("snobs", "tourists", "racists"), but it was only in recent years that I have actually made it out successfully.

I cruise along, free as a bird. A blackbird. Everything is going smoothly, until I decide to stop at Chester services for some food. As I'm driving along the entrance road I lose control of the vehicle and career left and right, but I manage to stick on the road and don't collide with anything. I drive into the car park and park up – between the white lines, as you're supposed to, even though it seems to be going out of fashion. I had assumed I had skidded on some oil, but when I get out, eager for some breakfast, I'm dismayed to see one of the rear tyres is flat. I've had a blow-out. I suddenly feel cold – that could have happened on the motorway at 70mph, but instead it happened at about 10mph on a quiet entrance roadway. My rumbling stomach has saved me.

I start to change the tyre, inserting the jack into the jacking-point and I begin winding it up. The van starts to rise, then there's a sickening crunching noise and the van sinks down again. The jack has gone through the corroded metal underside. I just stare. I have a horrible sinking feeling, fearing the worst, that this might be the end of Eagle One, due to her being structurally unsound. I need help. I need somebody. Not just anybody. I need the AA.

Fortunately, I'm a member, so I call them. I then go into the services to wait. In the toilets, there are posters over the urinals – adverts for you to read while you're otherwise engaged. The adverts are for motor insurance – I think. There is a quote from Sterling Moss: "There are two things a man won't admit he's not good at. Driving and making love." I chuckle out loud – not always a good idea when you're in the toilets. Another has a quote from someone else: "When driving look through the windscreen, not the rear-view mirror." Deep.

I eat a rather subdued breakfast then head back out to the car park, as the AA man is due. On exiting the services, I hold the door open for a man behind me and he says "Thanks, buddy!" with such gusto; it gives me such a glow of satisfaction, because so many people don't thank you. (I'm easily pleased.)

Within an hour a friendly Scouser, Dave, draws up in an AA van. He's able to jack the vehicle up using his floor jack and checks the situation regarding the vehicle's safety. Eagle One is undersealed, he tells me. I don't know exactly what that means, but it's obviously good. I think. The corrosion is not structural, he assures me. "You'd be better off getting a floor jack and just throw it in the back. You can get further under the vehicle than you can with your standard issue scissor jack." The van isn't big enough to "throw" large pieces of equipment in the back. And I'm in the AA, so I don't expect to *have to* "throw equipment in the back".

Dave lives nearby, just around the corner he says. He chats easily and I learn about A Day in the Life of Dave. He has four children and a trailer tent. By my reckoning, that's four children and a trailer tent too many. He talks about a recent holiday they've had to Dorset, but I'm just thinking: "With four children! That's not a holiday!

Four children! In a trailer tent! Four children! To Dorset!" It makes me wonder about other people's lives and the choices they make or have forced upon them. I've never wanted children – I've never seen the appeal and have always felt it was an extra problem in life I could do without.

Dave warns me to get out of the car park before my permitted two hours is up, shakes my hand and is gone. I have about eighteen seconds legally left in the car park, so I jump behind the wheel and start the engine.

* * * * * * * * * *

If Brendan was with me...

Oh, what fun we could have had a Crosby Beach. Brendan would have barked at each and every one of the Gormley statues and he wouldn't have been pacified. He would also have barked incessantly at Dave the AA man.

NOTES

#1: Apparently, the Cock & Seaman closed its portholes for the last time in 2018 and is no more.

#2: There is a chance that was a different Waterloo. There is also a chance that this one was named after that one. There is considerably less chance that that one was named after this one.

A metal cast of the artist, Sir Anthony Gormley - with no pants on.

CHAPTER 4: "ACROSS THE WATER"

In which I go "across the water", pass by effluent and the affluent, have afternoon tea, walk to an offshore island and hear the unmistakeable singing of seals... but mistake it.

It feels good to be up and running again, my wheels intact. I take a detour through the quaint little village of Ince, which was rural once, a lovely and remote country village, but is now surrounded by a landscape of pipes and silos belonging to the Stanlow Oil Refinery, which is the size of a small yet large town. Ince has become engulfed and strangled in a petro-chemical wilderness. On this occasion it smells of gas – and I'm pretty sure it usually does.

I'm trying to find the Ellesmere Port Boat Museum, but it isn't signed. However, I do find the Ellesmere Port Effluent Treatment Works, which *is* signed, which implies it is more popular. I hope not, because that's shit.

I'm somewhat lost. There are numerous tourist signs for retail parks, which are clearly how and where the masses prefer to spend their time these days. The old shopping streets of the town have many premises which are shuttered up and closed down. They probably couldn't take the competition from the retail parks. This is representative of Britain in general. Retail developments are the new temples. Religion is no longer the opium of the people – shopping is. Britain isn't so much a nation of shopkeepers, as shoppers.

I'm approaching the Wirral - an angular peninsular between Merseyside and Wales. It was traditionally in Cheshire, but since 1972 the majority of it comes under the Merseyside umbrella. Scousers consider the Wirral posh and refer to it as "across the water", meaning the Mersey estuary.

Many famous people have been born, grown up or lived here, including cricketer Ian Botham; Blond Bond, Daniel 007 Craig; acting politician, Glenda Jackson; deadpan broadcasting legend, John Peel; singer, songwriter and Buddy Holly impersonator, Elvis Costello; Professional and actor, Lewis Collins, and electronic musicians in the dark, Orchestral Manoeuvres, whose early material I'm listening to now, as it seems fitting.

I finally get to my destination – the Northern-most tip of the Wirral peninsula, New Brighton. Driving through the outskirts of the town is almost like driving through the back streets of Blackpool or some other seaside town, which isn't that odd, because that's exactly what New Brighton is... was... kind of was... or wanted to be... tried hard to be... but wasn't... and isn't (Sorry – it just *isn't*.)

Towards the latter part of the 19th Century, New Brighton was developed as a Regency-style coastal resort, intended for the genteel. It actually became the seaside for the mill folk of Manchester and Lancashire to spend their holiday times, their Wakes weeks and days off. They planned big when laying out the sea front of this town. There are wide parades, wide roads and parking for thousands of vehicles which will sadly never come. There are shelters in a vaguely 'Twenties/Art Deco style. It looks like a nice clean town – a seaside resort for the locals; no longer for holiday-makers.

In 1900, New Brighton Tower was built. Blackpool Tower had already opened a few years earlier – inspired by the Eiffel Tower. New Brighton Tower outdid its neighbour by being even taller, becoming the tallest tower in the country. Sadly, it was closed in 1919 after maintenance had been neglected during the First World War. By 1921 it was gone – dismantled, and largely forgotten – while Blackpool Tower, its stumpy neighbour – lives on.

Despite New Brighton being a seaside resort that has all but had its day as a seaside resort, I like it. I like the seaside out of season; there's something very atmospheric about a deserted promenade, the wind blowing, last season's paint peeling. I certainly prefer it to a weekend in the high season when there are people everywhere, doughnut fat, sticky children, the coconut smell of sun cream and countless flabby Brits beached and cooking nicely.

I park up. There are plenty of spaces along the wide prom. The brown, sandy sea is fully in and the waves are hitting the high sea wall with considerable force, sending up fine spray; it has immense power and watching the waves break is hypnotic.

It's high tide and the New Brighton lighthouse is stranded out in the water, where the Mersey and the sea become one. I once walked (and cycled along the road sections) the length of the Mersey, from my hometown in Stockport, all the way to this point. Touching the lighthouse was the symbolic end to my journey. While I was doing this, my bike was being stolen from where it was chained-up outside the ferry terminal in Liverpool. I suppose it has a cliched poetry to it.

Close by the lighthouse is Perch Rock Fort, built to protect the Port from attack by Napoleon. Remember, according to Abba he surrendered at Waterloo, which is directly across the Mersey, where Antony Gormley's statues stand as naked and nude as the day they were cast. Small world.

Perch Rock is no longer a working fort; it currently seems to be completely closed. A hastily painted sign at the entrance reads succinctly: CLOSED. There's nothing to say it will ever open its drawbridge again. When I last visited New Brighton on a rainy day in 2009, the fort was being used as a music venue; there were posters advertising forthcoming events, mainly bands that had their heyday in the 'Eighties... More nostalgia. New Brighton seems partly locked in the past somehow – a relic from a bygone age, probably a better age: a souvenir from the past. I don't mean that in a bad way – it seems to be half modern, half old, filled with a feeling of yesteryear, pulling it in two different directions between a modern Merseyside suburb and a Victorian seaside resort.

Actually, it's likely that New Brighton has given up the

ghost on the whole seaside thing. Where there was formally an open space next to the boating lake, there is now a new retail park. The arse-end of the complex is directed at the prom, so as you stroll past you can see the loading bays, offloading lorries, the bins, the extractor fans and the staff smoking. To me it completely ruins any claim New Brighton has or had to being a seaside resort. #1. Ironically, (like the sexed-up Blackpool Tower) the retail park probably attracts more visitors than the prom, lighthouse or fort ever did.

Down a side street, I find a lovely café called "Remember When Wirral". It's cosy and comfortable, like a traditional café used to be before everything went all American and Starbucksy. The café is filled with mementos from the past, cake stands, decorative tea pots and ornaments. The walls are covered with old black and white photographs of the area in its heyday and also a range of vintage posters, REMEMBER WHEN… YOU COULD GIVE A FLYING DUCK. (It shows three of those pottery flying ducks that were fashionable at one time – as featured in Hilda Ogden's house in Coronation Street.) The music is also vintage, the furious doo-wopping of the Four Seasons, led by the troubling falsetto of Frankie Valley, who was recommending we walk like a man. Although he may have walked the walk, he wasn't really talking the talk.

As if all that isn't enough, the café is staffed by the friendliest and loveliest ladies imaginable. The tea is proper leaf tea and gorgeous. I have a scone and then another scone… And because I'm supposed to be sort-of-dieting, I stop there, which takes some will power. (My usual maxim is: enough is as good as a feast, but more is even better.)

I wander back along the prom, enjoying New Brighton for what it actually is: a town by the sea rather than a seaside town. It still has a lot on offer and I like it. I stand for a while watching the surging waves hitting the sea wall, filled with regret… Not so much about life, or friends lost, or chances I was afraid to take, or a hundred other situations that would slide easily into the outline for a musical, but simply because I hadn't had a third scone.

* * * * * * * * * *

As I previously postulated, the eastern shore of the Wirral alongside the Mersey is assuredly Merseyside, in its location and its character. It's linked to Liverpool by the famous ferries 'cross the Mersey, which Gerry Pacemaker used because this land's the place he loves… and here he'll stay. (Although he has homes in Anglesey and the Costa Brava, he also has a place in Merseyside, so this makes him technically not a liar.)

There are also rail and road tunnels that pass beneath the river, linking Birkenhead with the City of Liverpool. Birkenhead is an industrialised town, previously famous for shipbuilding. It is less famous as the home of the first municipal park, which was the inspiration for New York's Central Park.

Previous industries on the Wirral included smuggling and "wrecking": enticing ships onto the rocks, so that the cargo could be plundered. Is that where the national identity of Scousers comes from? Although technically they're not Scousers here – they're "across the water" remember, though they definitely share a common accent.

Anyway, after some faffing about I arrive in Leasowe, a short way along the wreckers' coast, home to the first building in the world to be heated entirely by solar energy. Let me say that again... *in the world.* The "Solar Campus" is a 'Sixties comprehensive school, built to an ingenious design, whereby air is naturally heated by the sun. On the coldest days it is always 60 degrees Fahrenheit inside, and in summer the school remains cool. It is an ecological triumph of engineering.

I pitch up at my camping site on the gentrified side of the Wirral, outside the tiny village of Thurstaston. It is the most expensive site I have ever stayed on; I pay extra for electricity. It's very nice though and I have a partial sea view – the tidal Dee estuary. I head out for a walk before sunset. I stroll along the beach, feet crunching on the pebbles and shingle of the upper shore, beside an open expanse of sea, darkening clouds and grey mountains over the water. I suddenly realise this is quite a significant moment. I started this trip looking over an estuary into a different country: over the Solway Firth into Scotland; now I'm looking over the Dee estuary into Wales. It seems like a milestone.

The tide is going out and the sun is reflected in the wet sand. It's getting cold as the evening descends. I watch as the sun melts into the jagged horizon, setting with a burst of orange over the dark hills of Wales.

* * * * * * * * * *

On waking, there is still no rain, though the clouds are low and dark. I drive to one of the highest points on the Wirral, the mysterious Bidston Hill, a wooded hilltop, unspoilt and with a wealth of interesting things jammed amongst its trees. The rain is now here and is taking no prisoners. I sit in Eagle One watching it thrashing down, waiting for an appropriate lull, but I come to realise there isn't going to be a lull – appropriate or otherwise – and I just need to get out and get wet. So I get out – clad in waterproofs – and I get wet.

The terrain is partially flat rock underfoot, partially grassy, broadleaved woodland with shrubs and brambles and heathland. Even in the heavy rain, it's still a beautiful place. And even though the air is grey there's still a lot of colour, the yellow flowers of the gorse and the lime and lemon of the autumnal silver birch alongside brown, curling bracken.

The stationary sails of Bidston Windmill rise up into the colourless sky, still and silent. A short way further on, the white domes of Bidston Observatory come into view. One of its functions was to determine the exact time. It was also used to predict the tides for the D-Day landings. Right next door is the Bidston Hill lighthouse, built of local stone. The light is no longer active, but the lighthouse has also recently been carefully restored.

I startle a hardy little robin, who's having a bath in a puddle nearby. Even though he flies away as I approach, he flies back again when I've passed and continues his ablutions, determined not to be interrupted. I wonder why he's having a bath in the pouring rain. Even though it's a grey and dismal day – or perhaps *because* of it – he's turned the colour on his breast to maximum and it's a vivid and vibrant red.

A few steps away is one of the hill's most ancient features, the carving of a horse on an exposed piece of flat rock which is actually part of the footpath. There's no protection, so people continually walk on it; there has been no attempt to divert the footpath and reduce the footfall. Even worse, because it's so public and sandstone is so soft, graffiti-ists have been at work and carved their names in the rock and within the outline of the horse, which is a travesty.

Bidston Hill has legends of murders, satanists, a werewolf and UFOs. It also has fly tippers. Dumped: a set of rattan arm chairs and a matching settee. They look immaculate; the only thing wrong with them is that they're hideous, but I suppose they're quite fashionable in a retro and hippy sort of way. I'm sure someone would love them and pay good money for them. They've been carried a considerable distance to be dumped there – it would be easier to take them to a charity shop or donate them to the Salvation Army. This really pisses me off. A short way further on there's more household waste: furniture, kitchen items, a fridge and a microwave. This isn't the work of people who are on the verge of poverty and can't afford to have their rubbish removed, because these items have obviously been replaced with new stuff. They are just getting rid of their old crap. It says so much about a person – it's so much more than just dumping, it's saying they don't care about anyone else; they don't care about shitting on someone else's doorstep or ruining this beautiful place for other people.

I tramp along through the undergrowth, seething to myself until I come across a strange square structure, which is an air vent for the air raid tunnels that were burrowed deep under the hill. It was a vast network which was in use during World War II; they are now sealed for public safety, but opened occasionally for organised tours. It's rumoured that at one time these tunnels had linked the cellars of the local coven of witches, so they could have secret meetings without being spotted.

The last point of interest on the hill is a carving of a Sun goddess on an outcrop of rock: arms outstretched and an image of the sun at her feet. Although it's unprotected, unlike the horse it isn't directly on the path and is somewhat sheltered, so it has thankfully so far escaped graffiti and foot traffic, so it's better preserved and easier to see. It's believed to be of Norse origin, from around 1000AD.

Having not seen a soul for several hours, I decide it's time to go somewhere where there are people and get a bit of human colour. I drive to Parkgate on the Deeside of the peninsula. Like Grange-over-sands, it is a former port, but changes in tide and river left it high and dry, stranded behind marshes. Today, it's a very pleasant village facing the river.

I head to a pub in the middle of the village, very appealing on the outside but completely deserted on the inside; it has all the atmosphere of a graveyard – a really unpopular graveyard. I sit with my pint and look out over the marshes towards the hills of Wales. Now I'm finally inside, the sun comes out.

* * * * * * * * * *

A new day. A bright and sunny morning – as forecast. Because of the weather I have chosen this day to head out to Hilbre Island, the jewel in the Wirral's crown. Hilbre Island, or *islands* rather, as it's an archipelago, lies in the Dee estuary towards the top of the Wirral. The islands are completely cut off except at low tide, making them an isolated and very special place and an important nature reserve.

From the camp site, I head on foot along the Wirral Way – formerly a railway line linking West Kirby with Hooton which, as usual, had been closed by Dr Beeching in the 'Sixties. At this point, the line runs mainly through cuttings, so there are very few views, but the banks are decorated with colourful trees in their autumn colours – red berries beneath clear, blue skies. There are a number of birds making chirpy, up-beat bird-noises, but not a single one visible. For all I know it might just be a soundtrack.

I take a path that veers from the inland railway line and heads to the sandy beach, which is filled with people walking their dogs – all shapes and sizes. Lots of different dogs too. Everyone is friendly, smiles and says hello.

There is only one safe route across the wide estuary to the islands and already a line of brave pilgrims are striding out across the sand. I set off and more intrepid souls follow in my wake. It's beautifully sunny as I walk away from the coast, across the flat of the empty estuary. I can see the white tower of the beach lighthouse at Point of Ayr in Wales and out to sea there are dozens of wind turbines standing out against the horizon.

Hilbre Island is the largest of a group of three islands. Considering the island is supposed to be unlived-on now, there appear to be a number of houses in a very well-kept state. I read a few years ago that they were looking for a warden to live here, but couldn't find anyone willing to put up with a lack of mains water, electricity, proper sanitation and be cut off and isolated for hours every day. I think it sounds great! I found a web chat on a news site, with several angry people saying they hadn't seen the post advertised and would have loved to do it. The final comment was from an angry man who thought it was all a ploy by the council to save money by axing the warden's salary, hence they had only advertised it on a post-it note hidden under a door mat. That seems very likely to me.

On the final approach to the island, I come across two spritely ladies. Before my eyes, they both appear to start dancing; they're actually trying not to slip on the weed-covered rocks, but they fail and they fall. I dash over to offer help. They are both thankfully unhurt, just embarrassed.

"We don't want to fall again." Naomi says, "At our age we break easily."

As a result of this incident, we start talking and they tell me about the wildlife, especially the colony of seals. "Did you hear them singing a short while ago?" says Naomi's Friend. I hadn't. "You *didn't?* They make a whooo-whooo sort of noise."

Naomi points them out to me, basking on a far sandbank. They're just black dots. I had seen them earlier, but assumed they were a flock of sea birds.

"Do you have binoculars?" Naomi's Friend asks.

"I do..." They wait expectantly for me to sling my rucksack off. "But they're in my van."

They both roll their eyes. "Well, listen out for them. Remember, whooo-whooo."

They bid farewell and teeter off, up the sandy path to the main body of the island, but I bump into them at every point and it quickly gets embarrassing. I fear they suspect I'm stalking them, which I'm not.

There are amazing views in all directions. A 360 degree panorama, as far as the Great Orme's Head and way out to sea. I explore every inch of the island, especially the dwellings, which appear in very good condition and semi-lived in. Having left no stone unturned, I sit down in the soft, tufty grass for a rest, enjoying the sunshine and the sea breeze, feeling completely at peace and very happy to be here. I have wanted to visit for well over a decade and here I finally am, and it hasn't disappointed.

I love islands. I love the feeling of being cut off, isolated from society. That's largely – I think – where my love of lighthouses comes from. Part of me yearns for a simpler way of life, a subsistence lifestyle: days spent doing practical jobs like gardening and collecting firewood – good, honest labour that you benefit from directly. Although I feel Wirral Council probably *did* sneak the warden's post out of the back door to save money, I can't help wondering what it would be like to be on the island alone, when the tide is in and the day visitors have all gone. At night it might be quite eerie at first. I would miss Nicky, of course, though we have a very odd set-up. We don't live together and we have only ever seen each other for half a week, due to working odd hours and other commitments, so even though we live close-by we sometimes don't see each other for days on end.

I lie down in the sunshine. I genuinely feel so relaxed and contented. And then I hear the singing of the seals. It's a very odd cry, almost like children playing at ghosts rather half-heartedly. I wouldn't have known it was seals making that noise if it wasn't for Naomi and her friend. Right on cue, Naomi and Friend appear, seemingly having scaled the cliff. They laugh when they see me, in that we-must-stop-meeting-like-this sort of way. Really, we must! We do a bit of seal chat and then they disappear again.

I've been in a blissed-out state for what seems like twenty minutes; I'm so out of it that I nearly have to report myself missing. When I come round, I realise the sun has gone behind a grey cloud and it's a lot colder and getting quite windy. Apart from that, the island has gone eerily quiet. There's no one about. There had previously been a dozen or so visitors, which – on a very small island – felt busy. It suddenly feels unsettling. I wonder if I'd fallen into a deep sleep and missed the tide. I need to vacate by 12.30 and it's now 12.05, so I'm supposedly in good time, but even so I feel like I've been left behind and could be stranded on the island. (Part of me is hoping that's the case!)

I make my way back down to the beach and follow the

prescribed safe route across the bay, as the sky grows ever darker. I want it to rain as soon as I get back to Eagle One: rain like it really means it, because I want an excuse to relax inside for the rest of the day. It doesn't rain. Not a drop. But I stay in and relax anyway. Simply because I want to.

* * * * * * * * * *

Last day on the Wirral. Last port of call: a Victorian "garden village" Port Sunlight, built by soap magnate, William Lever, for the employees at his soap works. The name comes from their most popular brand of cleaning product, Sunlight soap.

Strolling around Port Sunlight is a sheer joy for me; it has many green open spaces, water-features and statues. I love architecture and there are so many different styles incorporated into the village, which contains an amazing 900 Grade II listed buildings. Nearly thirty architects were employed for the design work, which accounts for the great variety in styles. Within minutes I've clocked up everything from mock Tudor to Queen Anne and a shed-load in-between, all constructed very much with the sensibilities of the Arts and Crafts movement.

TV presenter, Fiona Bruce, grew up in Port Sunlight and singer Pete Burns was born here. I can see Fiona Bruce fitting in, poking around and looking for valuable antiques, but I struggle to picture Pete Burns sashaying down one of the tree-lined cul-de-sacs and getting his high heels caught in a grating, causing him to spin round like a record, baby.

Sitting in the middle of the village – rather like a spider in a web – is the Lady Lever art gallery, an impressive, white, classical building. Ignoring the art, I head downstairs to the tearoom. It's a room and there's tea in it, but that's about it. I'm surprised by what a functional canteen the café is, for such a grand building. It's underground, so windowless, and while the room itself might have some charm, it's rather ruined by the horrible and characterless plastic-topped tables.

I join the queue at the counter. There are only two people in front of me, but it becomes apparent fairly quickly that getting served is at least a half-day event. The queue behind me begins to grow; in response the sole girl serving begins to move slower and slower, as though she's clockwork and winding down. I wonder if she could possibly be more disinterested, but then one of the kitchen staff shuffles past and proves that disinterest and inertia can certainly be taken to even lower levels. When I eventually get my tea – about a week later – I wish I hadn't bothered.

I return to Eagle One for lunch, where there is an unfortunate incident with the tea towel. I won't go into details, but let's just say that due to user error it catches fire, but I manage to put it out without too much trouble. Waste not want not – the smouldering remains will be turned into cleaning cloths. (I might not have been alive during the war, but I have genetically inherited that "make do and mend" wartime characteristic; I can't stand waste. This might explain the wide selection of partially-charred cleaning cloths I have under my sink at home.)

I like Port Sunlight, but it's time to leave. I start the engine and drive away – with the windows open due to the smell of burnt cotton. I'm really looking forward to the next leg of my journey. As L.P. Hartley didn't say: "Wales is another country. They do things differently there."

* * * * * * * * * * *

If Brendan was with me...

I'm not sure Brendan would have appreciated the whooing of the seals on Hilbre, or the long walk out to the island. He would probably have liked Bidston Hill, because he does enjoy inspecting fly-tipping. He would especially have enjoyed stretching out in the deserted pub in Parkgate, with no one there to annoy him.

NOTES

#1. If you dare, Google Martin Parr's controversial book of New Brighton photographs *The Last Resort*, which caused a local outcry. It's unfortunate that New Brighton was the target, as it could apply to any British seaside town. It shows a less than flattering side of the British seaside, such as families sitting on concrete eating chips, surrounded by overflowing bins and litter.

ABOVE: Perch Rock Lighthouse, New Brighton, Merseyside.

ABOVE: The windmill, Bidston Hill.

CHAPTER 5: NORTH
BY NORTH WALES

In which I drive through Rhyl, but don't stop. I visit the "Queen of Welsh Resorts" and take a death-defying cablecar ride .

Wales welcomes me with open arms. Or at least a sign at the border saying "croeso i gymru". My mum's maiden name was Jones, so I'm practically local. Well, I can't actually speak Welsh or understand it; I did once try to learn it from a book, but it was much too complex. Thanks to place names though, I probably know more Welsh words than any other language after English.

I cruise along listening to Blondie, singing away and I'm very happy. I drive the old way to the North Wales holiday resorts, the way I remember from my childhood, before the A55 bypass was built. The towns are busy and as they're based along a main road they appear a bit shabby and dusty. There are lots of closed chapels and lots of closed pubs – both ends of the spectrum. According to research, a crate of supermarket lager and a huge, wall-mounted flat screen TV are currently the preferred and cheaper pastimes of the masses.

I get a flash and a hoot from an AA van coming the other way; I assume it's Dave the Scouser who had sorted my tyre. If it isn't, it's just an alarmingly friendly AA man, a man dangerously happy in his work, hooting and flashing at random.

I've been tailed for some way by a middle-aged couple in a silver Daimler Midlife Crisis convertible, both wearing oversized bobble hats, presumably to combat the severe cold and the wind chill factor of driving at speed and not being able to afford a roof. They follow me all the way into Talacre, a small seaside village in Flintshire. It was used by the military during the war, as an aircraft target range and also a testing site for anti-radar devices, resulting in - on occasion - the whole of the village being covered with silver foil. It seems to exist these days solely due to its proximity to the sea. It has caravan parks, bungalows, amusements, colourful beach shops with spinning windmills and day-glo beachballs, a chippy, bakery, café and pub. It is a seaside holiday resort in miniature. (Everything is normal-sized, you understand, there just isn't much of it.)

From the village, there is a boardwalk leading through the sandhills to the sea. Despite it being a cold and grey day, this walkway is busier than the M56 had been. There are many parents with gangs of very young kids. The average number of children per couple appears to be about twenty-eight and they race ahead towards the beach with excitement. One enterprising mother tries to slow her sons down by warning them that there are crocodiles and sharks on the beach, but they aren't fooled. However, I keep a wary eye out after that, just in case she's telling the truth.

The beach is wide and sandy and windy and it goes on

forever. Or further. This is the Point of Ayr, which to me always sounds Scottish. But it's not-ish. It's Welsh. A weak sun is trying valiantly to shine through thin clouds, but without success. There are views across to the Wirral and I can just about make out the windfarm amidst the hazy sea. The North Hoyle Offshore Wind Farm was opened in 2003. It was the UK's first major offshore wind farm and has thirty wind turbines.

Undeniably, the focal point of this open beach is the lighthouse, standing alone, marooned on the sands. If Toyland (as in Noddy) had a lighthouse (and maybe it does, I haven't done extensive research), then it would surely look like this. A tall, sturdy white tower capped with a red lantern. It's most odd. It looks like it's wearing a red beret.

Last time I visited, I was photographing the lighthouse when I noticed something strange on the balcony; I saw it out of the corner of my eye and for a moment it filled me with cold dread. It was humanoid in shape and appeared to be leaning on the balcony railings staring at me. It was standing stock still, not moving at all – and it was beginning to reflect the sunlight – in a way that a normal person really shouldn't. A close-up through my camera revealed it wasn't a real person at all, it was some sort of grinning cyborg – silver and quite chilling. I hadn't seen this on photos in books or websites, so I assumed it was a fairly recent addition. It was quite horrible and really spooked me, but I couldn't say why.

I later did painstaking Google research for over two minutes and discovered the "Metal Man" was a sculpture called The Keeper, placed on the balcony of the lighthouse in honour of the resident ghost, who allegedly appears in that spot frequently. The Keeper has now gone, back into the ether, and the balcony is empty.

A TV advert by a well-known paint company (no advertising here, folks) featured the famous Dulux dog galloping along the beach with the lighthouse in the background. The lighthouse has recently been sold, for £100,000.

After a quick lunch in Eagle One, I set off driving through the North Wales holiday towns, which is nicer than I'd thought it would be, better than I remembered from childhood trips. The road passes through Prestatyn, which seems pleasantly suburban. The arrival of the railways brought Victorian holiday makers in their droves and it became known as "Sunny Prestatyn" – probably not ironically at first.

Next along the coast is Rhyl. There are a lot of bungalows, a golf course and countless static caravan sites, so everything is very low and there seems to be a whole lot of sky. Grey sky, unfortunately. Again, it seems nice, clean, pleasantly suburban. I didn't realise it actually *was* Rhyl at first, because I didn't see a "Welcome to Rhyl" sign, which possibly means I'm not welcome.

Rhyl has also been a popular tourist destination since Victorian times. It started out as "charming" and "genteel" but over time it began to attract less charming and less genteel people; the Mancs and Scousers looking for somewhere with a beach where they could get pissed and pull a bird. Nowadays they probably flock to foreign climes, Ibiza or wherever happens to be "on trend" at the moment. But in those days – gangs of eager lads, gangs of easy lasses, bit of sunshine and you've got Grease the musical. Without the music.

Like so many seaside towns, Rhyl fell on hard times and everything that made it appealing to the tourist seems to have been systematically destroyed. The Marine Lake Funfair was demolished in the late 1960s. The pier – after a very ill-fated career of ships crashing into it, storm damage and fires, was finally demolished in 1972. The landmark Pavilion Theatre was demolished a year later. The Ocean Beach Funfair closed in 2007 and was demolished. The Skytower opened in 1989 but closed to the public in 2010.

In my teenage years, you *had to* go to Rhyl to visit the Sun Centre, an indoor swimming pool with water flumes and a wave machine. You didn't do anything else in Rhyl, as even then it had a reputation as a dump. I was surprised to read it had closed in 2013. With all these closures what exactly is left in Rhyl to attract the tourist? I suspect *nothing*. It has a drug problem and a growing number of unemployed people have moved here to live in DSS B&B accommodation and hostels. This greatly angers the local people, who see their once-prosperous town overrun by "layabouts and scroungers".

I eventually find my way through the arse-end of Rhyl – and my good feeling from the morning starts to evaporate. I love the sea, hate the seaside, which usually means a concrete town that smells of deep frying. Oceans of bungalows. A sea of static caravans. A wave of frying food. Chips. Beached families with too much exposed, singeing flesh. A tide of hot, sticky children.

Hot sticky tarmac. The sickly-sweet, fatty smell of "fresh" doughnuts. Chips. The hectic flashing of amusement arcades. The piped music of fairground rides. The gaudy pink of candy floss... I'm not knocking other peoples' holiday choices... Well, clearly I am, but this isn't for me. This is hell with a side order of chips. This is chips with a chip garnish.

Our old friend the Knowhere Guide lists many issues by Rhyl locals, who are all united in their loathing of the unemployed incomers: "Scum from the cities with their drug, social problems... GO HOME...WE DON'T WANT YOU HERE!!!!!!!!", "Bedsits and the horrible 'non-contributing people to the town'...GO HOME, YOU ARE NOT WANTED HERE!!!!!" Either Rhyl locals are very fond of their exclamation marks, or those two were penned by the same person!!!!! And my favourite, which starts off sounding like a rather prim handwritten complaint to the letters page in the Daily Mail: "The state of the prom is absolutely disgusting. It hardly says "Come and visit Rhyl" It actually says "Piss here!" It's a disgrace."

The late Steve Strange, most famous as the kleptomaniac frontman of 'Eighties New Romantic pop group Visage, lived here for many years as a child. His parents ran a boarding house. Visage had a few electronic hits then faded to grey.

Liver Bird, Nerys Hughes, was born here, but the town's most infamous daughter was Ruth Ellis, the last woman to be executed in the United Kingdom. On Easter Sunday 1955, she shot her lover dead, then commendably turned herself in to the police. She was found guilty and hanged.

A lot of money has been poured into Rhyl recently to make it better and more appealing to the visitor. I have decided I'm going to attempt to find three things worth visiting Rhyl for.

Driving through the town, there are lots of closed and vacant shops, but it's a similar situation in virtually every town. The shops that *are* open look very uninviting. The people in the streets – they may be locals, they may be visitors, I don't know – all look grim-faced and aggressive. Something has gone very wrong in the centre of Rhyl. I don't see anything nice at all. Nothing. I'm sure there *are* good things, great things even, but I don't see them.

On a positive note, there is a lot of building going on in the town and close to the seafront: hoardings everywhere, demolitions and recently demolished spaces. It implies Rhyl is having a makeover. I hope it's successful, but it will take a lot of work and ingenuity to regenerate this sad town.

* * * * * * * * * * * *

It's only a fairly short drive along the coast to Rhos-on-Sea, which is a complete contrast to Rhyl; a nice seaside town, with not much going on, but not much wrong with it. The road winds around the Little Orme and into Llandudno, the "Queen of the Welsh Resorts", a title first used in 1864. It is now the largest seaside resort in Wales. The first thing I notice is the huge "Welcome to Llandudno" sign, which is very welcoming... and a sign.

I park at the far northern end of the bay, next to a blue-painted paddling pool. It's cold and windy and the pool is empty and out of use. Nevertheless, it feels like a seaside town *out of season*, not a seaside town *out of date*. Close by is the modern, newly-built Lifeboat Station. LLandudno was the only town in the UK to have its previous lifeboat station located in the middle of town, so it was equidistant from both of its shores. When called into action, a launch would typically take between 12 and15 minutes, which is a long time if you're drowning. A new boathouse was completed in the summer of 2017 and a new boat arrived in the autumn.

The town got its name from its patron saint, Saint Tudno, who was a missionary from Cardigan Bay, who came to bring Christianity – and cardigans – to the heathen locals. I don't know much about missionaries, except the position, but Tudno sounds like a fine man. He lived in a hermitage on the Great Orme.

I walk almost the full sweep of the bay. It's mainly pebbles on the top of the beach with the sand lower down, currently concealed by a very laconic sea. Everywhere is grey, due to the overcast day; there is very little colour, but it feels nice. Llandudno has got it right; this is how to do *seaside*; it is *traditional* seaside. Seaside by its very nature is traditional and Llandudno embraces the traditional without whoring itself. There is still a Punch and Judy show in the summer months. It's good, old fashioned, harmless fun, fun, fun, as Mr Punch beats his wife and everyone in sight with his stick and tells us "That's the way to do it". So it's aiming to be instructional as well.

Amongst the notable features of the town are the pastel-painted hotels along the front and the elegant Victorian pier against the dramatic backdrop of the Great Orme. The Pier was built in 1878 and is the longest in Wales. There is tatt in Llandudno, of course, such as amusement arcades and doughnut and candy floss stalls on the pier, but they're in the attractive wooden kiosks, they're in the right place and they look classy and in-keeping.

One of the complaints on the Knowhere Guide website is that there are too many old people. And yes, it's always been popular with older folks. It's a traditional seaside town and the majority of it is flat and accessible, with everything you need within easy reach. *Of course*, it's popular with older people! It doesn't mean it has to be exclusively for them though. Looking around, I can see a large number of older people and several times have nearly been mown down by purple-rinsed adrenaline junkies making merry with mobility scooters. It makes quite a refreshing change to being nearly run-down by boy-racers.

I take a leisurely stroll along the pier, looking over the railings at the swelling sea below and the iron supports disappearing into the surging water. It's cold and breezy and the thin light is already beginning to fade, so I phone a campsite and book myself in. It's in the hills above Llandudno Junction, so I use SatNav Sally to show me the way. I should have known better. Her first instruction is to turn left from the prom road... into the sea. This is getting repetitive. What is her problem with the sea! I don't comply, so she changes her mind.

"Recalculating! Recalculating! Turn *right*." Even that's wrong. The driving is quite stressful as I'm taken down every single-track lane in the Llandudno area, requiring considerable negotiation with oncoming vehicles. (I find out later there is a very easy and direct route, which she seemed to be ignoring at all costs. The journey took me forty minutes, when it should have taken in the region of four.) On the positive side, I get to see an area of countryside I haven't seen before and there are good views over Llandudno. When I arrive at the small site it's completely dark. It's nice and rural, despite a view of the A55 dual carriageway in the valley below. Still, the owner is really friendly and he has good recycling bins, so I'm able to off-load all the cans and cardboard I've been carrying with me – always a cathartic experience.

The wind is picking up as the evening wears on and it's an exposed spot, so Eagle One rocks dramatically, which is great. I love dramatic weather.

* * * * * * * * * * * *

It's a rather grey morning, but there's no rain yet. I'm in no hurry to move on, as there is a lot to see in Llandudno. At 10am, I'm parking up at West Shore. Llandudno has two shores, one more famous than the other and with all the tourist features, while the West Shore is fairly quiet. There's a nice beach with spectacular views across the wide bay towards Anglesey and Puffin Island, but not much else. It is a largely residential area. It was here that Alice Liddell, later better known as *Alice in Wonderland* – though not to her face – spent the long Victorian summers of her childhood.

The Great Orme dominates Llandudno. It's a prominent limestone headland, formed on the bed of an ancient sea, then Ice Ages and volcanic action forced the rocks up out of the earth. The peninsula has been used by humankind since the Stone Age.

There are several easy ways to the top of the Great Orme: driving, the tramway and the cablecar, but if you ask me, by far the best way is on foot, so I set off along a footpath. The path splits and I choose the steeper one, thinking it will probably be shorter, will get me warmer quicker and will offer the best views of the sea. The path begins to ascend fairly gently at first. I pass several outcrops of the shrub, cotoneaster, with its blood red berries and small leaves: this is quite different from the regular garden variety and is apparently unique to the Orme.

There is a craggy cliff face towering over me. I spot what I take to be Kamikaze sheep, perched high on impossible ledges. How did they get there and how are they going to get down? They don't look worried though, happily grazing on tufts of grass that grow from fissures in the rock. In fact, they seem quite contented. When I get nearer, I realise they are in fact goats. They look a bit gruff: horn-ed beasts with beards blowing in the strong breeze. There are apparently several herds of these wild Kashmiri goats living on the Orme, supposedly descended from goats given by Queen Victoria to Lord Mostyn, who owned and built the town and everything around. Goats have a historic connection to witchcraft, possibly due to their demonic-looking horns, but these little grass-munchers look angelic if anything. Apart from the completely black one, which is probably the head of the local coven.

I pass a man with a German shepherd the size of a small horse and ask him how far it is to the summit. "It's about 600 metres." he tells me. "Ya." the shepherd agrees. After they've gone, I wonder whether he meant 600 meters in *paces* or 600 metres in *altitude*... There's quite a difference. The path isn't easy to follow and I end up taking a very long route and losing some height. As I near the top, the cablecar line comes into view, transporting the little coloured, open gondolas up and downhill. As far as I can remember, I've never been on a cablecar in my life and this is the longest single-stage cabin lift in Britain. I decide today will be the day I go on one.

Towards the Orme summit, the cablecar line passes directly overhead and I can hear every word the people in the gondolas are saying. It's mainly parents with young children. One dad thoughtfully says: "Look, there's a graveyard!" as though trying to make his offspring aware of their mortality and prepare them for the cruelty of life.

I'm soaked with sweat when I reach the top and touch the Trig Post, which stands at 679 feet. There are views in all directions, but it all looks rather dull and grey today, which is a shame. As the sweat cools, I start to feel very cold, so I don't spend too long looking at the ashen vista, but head inside the Summit Complex.

Originally, there had been a telegraph station on the site, which was part of a Georgian network of 11 stations between Liverpool and Anglesey, covering a distance of 80 miles. The present Edwardian building replaced it in 1909, as a golf club house, later becoming the Telegraph Hotel. During the Second World War, it was used by the RAF as the Great Orme Radar Station. Despite being built as a golf club house, it looks much as I'd expect a telegraph station to look, with an octagonal tower at one end, reminiscent of a lighthouse. It's busy, but not heaving. The bar is closed but the café is open and about half full. It's weirdly old fashioned, with those plastic cupboards containing food, where you lift up a flap to retrieve a piece of cake. The gift shop boasts in big letters: GIFTS FROM AROUND THE WORLD! Mainly Taiwan I'd imagine, judging by the cheap crap they seem to be flogging.

All over the walls, there are posters and newspaper accounts of a boxing champion called Randolph Turpin. In 1952, the complex was bought by Turpin and became known as Randy's Bar. Less than a decade later, Turpin was facing financial ruin after receiving a back-dated Income Tax demand, so he sold the complex. Since then, the hotel has continued to be associated with him, despite the fact that in 1966, aged 37, Turpin shot his daughter in the head and heart, then somehow did the same to himself. While he was killed, his daughter miraculously survived. It seems odd to have all these celebratory news cuttings on display and to venerate a man who was (by intent) a murderer.

I buy a very nice Americano and sit looking out of the window at the grassy plateau of the Orme. There is fairly awful piped music playing. A Beach Boys cover comes on, *I Get Around*, one of my favourites of their songs, covered here so badly and with some of the words wrong; it's excruciating.

The Great Orme is sprawling on top – you could walk for miles, but I'm keen to get on the cablecar. It's lucky I choose to go there now, as they're planning to close shortly, due to the wind expected to increase to dangerous levels. This news doesn't exactly delight me.

There are three particularly cantankerous old ladies in front of me and I'm concerned I'm going to be put in their cabin to make up a foursome, but it never arises. I'm installed in a little coloured gondola on my own, open to the elements. I'm flung out into the open air; that's the most adrenaline-pumping part, leaving the terminus and juddering out onto the cable. It's very windy and very cold.

The Great Orme Cabin Lift opened in 1969, but they are very quick to point out it was completely refurbished in 2006. The entire length is just over a mile. The gondolas travel at a heady 6 mph. Alarmingly, I seem to be gaining on the three old ladies in front. It's quite worrying when your car goes over the pylons that support the cable. There is quite a bit of juddering and you can't help wondering if you'll come off the wire and plummet to a messy demise. I had read the previous night about a woman who had jumped to her death from one of the cabins at the route's highest point, witnessed by stunned holiday-makers on the dry-ski slope. A verdict of suicide was later recorded.

The cablecar doesn't provide the best view of Llandudno – you see more of the rooftops and backstreets. It does, however, afford great views of the pier and out to sea. It's a memorable experience. Old fashioned, quaint, retro: call it what you will, but people have been enjoying this amenity for fifty years... and I hope they continue to do so.

* * * * * * * * * * * *

I go into a renowned chippy for lunch and eat in the cafe, chips and peas accompanied by a pint of lager. It's now

a gloriously sunny afternoon. Being British, everyone in the café comments on it. "What a glorious afternoon!"
I'm quite full and lazy after eating, so I dawdle along the high street, stroll along the prom the walk back across the peninsula to the West Shore via lovely back roads. I don't know if it's fatty food, alcohol or sunshine, or a cunning combination of all three, but I'm walking along seemingly in slow motion, almost in a trance of contentment. So far I've had a great day.

Before leaving the town, I undertake the "Marine Drive", which is a toll road that runs around the perimeter of the Great Orme. I get a rush of excitement as I drive up, because it looks like the tollbooth is unmanned and it looks like I'm not going to have to pay, but then a woman appears at my window from nowhere and lifts my toll fee of three pounds sterling from me. For a moment I'm gutted, but she's so jolly and lovely I would gladly keep handing her money for the rest of the afternoon.

From the Marine Drive, the views out to sea are amazing. The sea is slate green, and almost still from here. The off-shore wind farm is catching the sun; it all seems like an endless summer's day. The sheer cliffs, that drop down from the road to the sea, provide an ideal nesting environment for a variety of sea birds, including cormorants, guillemots, shags, razorbills and puffins, plus many others too numerous to mention. Of these, I can only recognise puffins and cormorants. Oh, and I know a shag when I see one.

Around the western side of the Orme, the foundations of an extensive military camp are visible. This was the site of the wartime Coast Artillery School and is now a scheduled monument. There was also a secret experimental radar station here, but you didn't hear that from me.

As the road rounds the Orme, there are breathtaking views over the bay towards Anglesey and the mountains of the mainland. The sun is glinting off the sea. It's beautiful and feels wide open; it's like being on the top of the world and gives a startlingly different view of an area I know well. The Marine Drive is well worth every penny of that three Welsh pounds I paid.

* * * * * * * * * *

If Brendan was with me...

I wouldn't have experienced the cablecar ride. I have heard that dogs are permitted, but Brendan would not have permitted himself. We've learned the hard way that he doesn't like odd travel, like boats, sea tractors and anything that leaves the ground... or moves in any way... He would point blank have refused to get onboard. He would have quite enjoyed the Marine Drive, but mainly because it would have meant he could curl up in his basket in the back of the van and ignore everything outside the window.

ABOVE: Point of Ayr lighthouse, Talacre, North Wales.

ABOVE: The pier, Llandudno

CHAPTER 6: YNYS MON:
THE ISLE OF THE DRUIDS

**In which I circumnavigate
the last Druid stronghold –
anticlockwise. I relive some
happy memories... well,
memories anyway... and visit the
king of all lighthouses. Possibly.**

I love Wales. The A55 bypass sneaks under the
Afon Conwy, bypassing the fortified town of Conwy
itself, which used to be a terrible bottleneck; it then
skirts the coast, weaving backwards and forwards and
passing through various tunnels beneath the quarried
mountains. There are tantalising glimpses of Anglesey
and its little satellite, Puffin Island, but there's not
enough time to gawp if you want to remain on the
carriageway.

The A55 takes you across the Menai Straits via the "new
bridge", the Pont Britannia – or Britannia Bridge if you
prefer. It was built by Robert Stephenson in 1850 to carry
the Holyhead railway line. In 1980, it was augmented to
carry the A55 as well. I always find it thrilling travelling
across the Straits, a fast flowing and dangerous stretch of
water that separates the island from the mainland. Far
below there is an amazing view of the graceful lines of the

"old bridge", *Pont Grog y Borth*, or the Menai Suspension Bridge, designed by Thomas Telford and completed in 1826. It is quite rightly a Grade I listed building. Prior to the construction of this bridge, Anglesey was an island-proper and the only contact with the mainland was by ferry.

The Isle of Anglesey, Ynys Mon in Welsh, was the last stronghold of the Druids, who were eventually massacred by the Roman army in AD61. The sacred groves where they worshipped were razed to the ground. It is generally accepted that the modern so-called "Druids" have considerably less claim to the name than my pants do.

I first came here as a child and – despite not being a Druid – I have loved it ever since. So, here I am, driving round the island in anti-clockwise fashion, because I can. Therefore, my first port of call is Beaumaris, a small, tasteful old town on the Straits. It has a castle, a compact high street with gift shops and cafes, the fascinating town gaol and boat trips to Puffin Island and elsewhere. It also offers unspoilt views across the water to the mountains of Snowdonia. It is lovely and unspoilt, despite being very popular.

Beyond Beaumaris, the road swings tightly to the north-eastern tip of Anglesey, a peninsula called Penmon Point, but there is a toll to pay for the last stretch. I barter with a chap about staying overnight and we come to an arrangement; he charges me an extortionate rate and I reluctantly pay him. It's a fiver on entry today and a fiver on exit tomorrow, as it's a fiver to pass per day, he reasons. This is *literally* highway robbery.

Eagle One bumps and jars along the toll road. I cling to the wheel, wondering why I've been charged quite a lot of money to knacker my suspension. The road terminates at Penmon Point, AKA Black Point or Trwyn Du in Welsh. The place of many names. There is a small car park and a rocky beach. On the outcrop of rocks, surrounded by the sea, stands Trwyn Du Lighthouse. It was built in the 1830's and has broad black and white bands and is very photogenic, but the best thing about Trwyn Du is its haunting bell, which chimes a slow, low, funereal note every twenty or so seconds. It's so eerie and atmospheric.

The lighthouse guards a treacherous, fast-flowing channel between Penmon Point and Puffin Island. Many ships have been lost in this area; indeed, the whole of the Anglesey coast is a graveyard of sunken vessels. I used to be very interested in diving when I was young and it was an ambition to visit these wrecks. Fortunately, that ambition passed with age.

The car park is quite full when I pull in, but five minutes later, by the time my kettle has boiled, there has been an exodus and only two cars remain. I could get paranoid about this.

There is so much to delight here, so much to explore. I love the whitewashed cottages, the lighthouse, the solemn bell, the island. I love the views over the bay, back to the distinctive bulk of the Great Orme, where the last rays of the sun are setting. The sky is tinted with lilac and indigo. The sun slips below the landward horizon and darkness falls. The two remaining vehicles exit the car park and I'm left completely alone.

There is an almost-full moon and the cloudless sky is filled with stars; there is very little light pollution so nothing obscures the heavens. After I've eaten, I'm cold and tired, so I have a lie down. I fall asleep immediately and awake in a muted, empty silence, which is punctuated rhythmically by the melancholy tolling of the lighthouse bell. I have slept solidly and feel refreshed. I reach for my phone to check the time. I have slept for – wait for it – a full hour. Though it feels like the stillness of the small hours, it is in fact 7.30pm.

I go for a short moonlit walk, accompanied by the solemn chiming, the steady blinking of the lighthouse lamp and the gentle lapping of the waves. Everything is strangely, hauntingly still, so atmospheric and so beautiful: an ethereal moonlit landscape.

There are no other camper vans here yet. I was hoping a van or two would come; there's safety in numbers. There is also some bizarre comfort knowing that if you're going to be murdered in the night then you won't be the only one.

* * * * * * * * * * * *

It's cold, it's grey, it's raining. It's Anglesey. I have to smile when I open my curtains and see raindrops speckling the window, because it reminds me of so many family holidays here. Summers were generally proper summers then, but we had friends who owned a bungalow here, so we came out of season a lot as well. We – me and Nicky – have had many holidays here since, usually in June for my birthday. It has normally rained then as well. I'm happy for it to rain today. If I saw Anglesey in the sunshine, I'd probably think I'd taken a wrong turn.

The car park is empty. The sea is fully in. The lighthouse bell tolls. A big SUV-type vehicle pulls in, the driver gets out and gives me a dirty look. I've paid a lot to stay here, so he can piss off. I stay in bed for warmth and have a cup of tea. I'm in no hurry to leave, because when I do I'll have to pay another fiver to the toll man. It's still early when I set off. I secretly hope he might not be there yet. But he is there and he's gone a bit Scouse-sounding today, though his hat is distinctly Australian. "No morning photographers today." he says, "Usually there's several. Just you, wasn't it? All on your own."

"Yes... I had a very quiet and peaceful night."

He grunts. "Wish I had! But I've got a wife at home!"

I laugh and drive off, continuing anti-clockwise around the island. Green fields, nice villages: the rural interior of Anglesey. I arrive at Din Lligwy, the remains of a Romano-British settlement. It's a short walk across a field to the remarkably well-preserved, low, white stone remains of square and circular huts. The site is surrounded by trees which make it feel like a secret location, shrouded in mystery. It's such an impressive monument to the people who built these houses and lived here. I wander around, completely alone, enjoying the solitude. I'd like to stay longer, but I'm conscious of the daylight hours ticking away.

I drive a short way around the coast to the pleasant village of Llaneillian, which nestles at the end of a series of narrow lanes. It consists of a church and a few nice houses and some air – nothing more. It's along a dead-end road, so it gets no passing traffic. There is a small car park: open – and a toilet block: closed. A stroll downhill takes you to Porth Eillian, an inlet where the spurs of the coast form a naturally sheltered harbour. It's a sleepy and unspoilt little corner of Anglesey. I've been here several times in the past and hardly ever seen anyone about. It seems almost locked in another time.

There are good views towards the headland, Point Lynas, crowned by a conglomeration of angular white buildings, which make up the lighthouse. I follow the driveway, which has picturesque views in both directions along the dramatic coastline. It's as attractive as any coast in Britain. The sea is calm, a mixture of slate green and slate blue, but ultimately slate. A couple of big ships cruise slowly towards the horizon. Sea birds glide effortlessly over the clifftops and out to sea. It's an idyllic scene. I walk between heather and flowering gorse; I rub one of the yellow flowers and immediately it releases a rich, sweet scent reminiscent of coconut.

The tip of the headland, near the castle-like lighthouse is a well-known spot for spying seals, porpoises and dolphins. I scan the turbulent waters for some time, but can't see anything, except a tiny bird, which flies in front of me and settles in a hedgerow. He's a beige colour and wren-shaped, so I'm going to assume he's a wren. He's flitting from branch to branch making a sweet trilling noise, happy with his lot in life. And coincidentally, that's exactly how I feel: contented and at peace, but much larger than a wren. I haven't felt this sort of peace in a long time, but being out in the open, in the sea breeze, revisiting some familiar places and discovering new ones is something that agrees with me. I'm intensely enjoying it. I'm not coming to any conclusions about what I want from life, other than *this*; this peace, this tranquillity and this freedom. I identify with this happy little bird, who's called Gavin, which admittedly is a rubbish name for a bird.

I walk back to the car park. A man mowing the grass strip along the lane smiles and says: "How do." You sometimes expect people in isolated little communities to be hostile to interlopers, but I have – so far – only encountered friendliness in Wales.

I sit in Eagle One eating lunch – avocado on toasted sourdough bread with a salad garnish – with the side door open as it's so pleasantly warm. My view is of a garden across the car park, with many shrubs and trees surrounding it. I realise after some time that there are two gardeners at work, one on the lawn and one up a tree trimming the top. I have always been interested in plants and especially trees. As a child I took over my dad's vegetable patch and grew vegetables – what child does that? I've always thought it would be nice to be a gardener, because I like the idea of a simple life tending nature, growing plants and nurturing them, but I've always been put off by the negative side, the weeding, the pruning, the tree surgery.

The older gardener stands with his hands on his hips, looking up into the tree. "Alright, Jamie?"

The tree shakes and shivers, then I hear: "Shit. Shit! Ohhh shit!" accompanied by the sound of small, brittle twigs snapping.

The older man looks alarmed, hopping from foot to foot, but there's nothing he can do. The tree goes very quiet and still.

"Jamie?" he asks tentatively. "Jamie? Are you OK?"

Jamie has somehow managed to save himself and comes into view, climbing down his ladder. He's only young, though his hairstyle isn't. (Carbon-dating has since revealed it was from the early-Duran period, circa 1981.)

Crisis avoided, I leave Llaneilian via the narrow lanes, nearly plowing into an old granny who was standing in the middle of the road around a tight bend. She has a toddler with her, presumably her grandson, playing in a toy car. *In the road! On a tight bend!* She looks at me, mildly surprised to see a vehicle. (On a road! A vehicle... A *moving* vehicle... *on a road*!) I'm fortunately driving at a very *araf* (slow) speed and with the diesel engine growling she should have heard me. She catches my eye, nodding towards the kid with a: "Tsk! Kids today." sort of half-smile, but makes no attempt to move the kid out of the road. Shaking my head, I drive around them. Then reverse over her. (She needed to be taught a lesson.)

I pass through the town of Amlwch, which seems a bit dusty – and through Bull Bay, which is full of bungalows, then Wylfa, which is dominated by the huge square bulk of its nuclear power station, which was recently decommissioned. I eventually make it onto the A55, which is Anglesey's aorta. I drive across the bridge that links Anglesey with Holy Island, then through the backstreets of Holyhead, where everything seems to be pebble-dashed. Holyhead ("Drugs", "It's a bit drab", "Rain, dogshit, drunks, charity shops", "the pebbledash") is famous as being a port, with ferries to Ireland. It is less famous as being the birthplace of the French half of French and Saunders. It's not really famous for much else, except for being a bit grotty. I'm afraid I couldn't see much to contradict that view.

Once I've made it out of the dowdy suburbs, the landscape suddenly opens out, tree-less, wind-ravaged and harsh. It reminds me of the Scottish Highlands. The land ends suddenly at sheer cliffs that drop into the wide expanse of a seemingly endless ocean, stretching away towards a hazy and uncertain horizon.

South Stack is known for its lighthouse and its cliffs, which are a haven for seabirds and birdwatchers alike. It is closely guarded by the RSPB, who have an observatory on the cliff edge and a shop and information centre close by. I'm surprised to find the car parks are all quite full and the ice cream man is doing a steady trade, judging by the white-mouthed passers-by, jamming cones into their faces. As soon as I turn into the car park, huge drops of rain start to hit the windscreen, but I won't be deterred.

It's cold, grey and breezy. There are views from the cliffs, towards the Llyn Peninsula: jagged peaks lightly shrouded in mist. Shafts of sunlight slant down on the horizon from behind the clouds. Best of all, the lighthouse comes into view, far down below on its island, the sea thrashing around it. It is connected to the mainland by a metal bridge, which replaced an earlier rope bridge.

With some alarm, I realise it's 3.30 and I haven't had a tea or coffee since 7am, so I make a beeline for the café. I have a nice coffee sitting next to the semi-steamed window, with a partial view of the sea. Again, I'm struck that this is exactly what I love doing. It's not the "getting there" that's important, it's the journey. I am currently loving the journey.

* * * * * * * * * * * *

A short walk along the clifftop path, takes me through gorse and other low shrubs, providing a rich environment for butterflies, birds and other small animals. The path leads to the Holyhead Iron Age hut circles, a grassy location on the gentle, lower slopes of Holyhead Mountain. This is an amazing site, older and more isolated than Din Lligwy, but less hidden, more exposed and scoured by sea winds. It is an open, grassy site, surrounded by bracken. It has a strong atmosphere and is excellently preserved.

It's amazing to think that these low walls were built so long ago by human hands and that they have survived. One of the huts appears to have a crude fireplace and another to have a stone water bowl. The site is soaked in history and *you can actually walk amongst it.* There are round huts that would probably have been family dwellings and square huts that may have been stables, workshops or storage rooms. Roman coins were found in one of the huts, which suggests the village was lived in for nearly a thousand years.

Walking back along the cliffs, which face roughly west,

I'm eagerly anticipating a sunset over the sea, but the sun appears to have worn itself out. The light is fading, the colour is going and it's getting quite cold. Then, without any further messing about, the sun has gone – no spectacular sunset – it just blinks out like a light.

Back at the car park, the ice cream van has scarpered. With the café closed and the sun below the horizon, most people have left for their static caravans or warm hotels. The staff from the lighthouse have gone home and it has been left unchaperoned. The footbridge is locked and barred, so the island is, to all intents and purposes, a proper island again, populated only by the sea birds and the ghosts that live there.

Night time is settling over the land and the sea. Three intrepid camper vans remain in the car park in the fresh darkness. I feel a great comfort knowing there are other people camping here. (This only falls apart when one of the vans contains a murderer.) Although none of us speak, it feels like a community and there is (seemingly) safety in numbers. The van closest to mine contains a man who is evidently a bird watcher and keen photographer and has the hardware to prove it. The other van has a hippie vibe to it, with purple tinted windows. It seems to house a young couple, two dogs and an older person of indeterminate gender with a shock of white hair. It feels so much safer than the previous night at Penmon Point.

I have wild camped near here in a tent a few times, but always with one or more friends, so it has never felt in any way threatening. I'm all for people wild camping, as long as they choose a discreet spot and are considerate, leaving no trace of their stay.

The last time I stayed here, in this car park, was nine years ago. It was my first van, first trip and first time trying to park up and sleep overnight without the comfort and security of a campsite. That was how I planned to use my van. I loved the idea of basically always being at home, of being able to pull up anywhere, in any layby or car park and stay the night. In reality, it isn't that simple at all. Firstly, there are by-laws in each area and the police often move you on. Here though, there are no such by-laws and although the police drive by occasionally, they don't seem to hassle you. What *was* an issue back then, was the peculiarly British pastime of "dogging".

Dogging: where couples or individuals meet up, often in rural car parks, for group sex. The last time I stayed here, several cars drove in, honked their horns, flashed their lights, waited a short while and then drove off. Several times throughout the evening, a police car drove into the car park, did a slow circle and then drove off again, which I found quite comforting. I hardly slept that night. Each time I heard a car engine, I was peering through a crack in the curtains. Sometimes it was doggers, sometimes it was the police car. I was on edge all night.

This time, I just feel privileged to be in such a beautiful spot and to experience this amazing and dramatic landscape after hours, when most people are tucked up in their beds. Or someone else's bed. Or spread-eagled on the bonnet of an Austin Allegro in the car park of a local beauty spot or sports centre.

In the night, I hear several cars driving past, but as I

had my van neighbours, I'm not remotely concerned. I let them get on with it. I go to sleep and I sleep well.

* * * * * * * * * * * *

I wake up at South Stack... which is good, because that's where I went to sleep. It's quite cold, but not freezing. It's a grey, static day. It isn't raining and there's no wind as such, just a grey, still, anaesthetised day with low, heavy clouds. The three vans have stayed all night and sit silently now, with steamed up windows. The photographer is the first to emerge; he's out early waving his unfeasibly large telephoto lens at unsuspecting seabirds.

I walk down the lane to the café, which isn't open yet, so I set off up Holyhead Mountain. Small birds are swooping low over the rocks and heather, changing direction at right angles and flying as one, in perfect synchronicity. They look strangely false, like badly done CGI, as dodgy as the CGI *Titanic* in that film... I forget what it was called.

Holyhead Mountain is only a hill really, but it's unmistakeable, as it's the largest and highest point on Holy Island and for miles across Anglesey. Its top is bare rock, very distinctive, gently arched. Its lower slopes are all rock and heather. Hi-viz workmen with cranes are erecting a mobile phone mast on the lower slopes. There are a few masts here already: a sign of the times. Possibly because I'm looking at the scenery, I suddenly see the ground rushing towards me. I've twisted my ankle and fallen over fully, so I'm sprawled on the ground. All I can think, regardless of the searing pain, is "I hope the workmen didn't see!" I've grazed both my hands in various places, but my main concern is my ankle; ankles can break and sprain notoriously easily. I'm able to stand up gingerly and put my weight on it. I continue walking – and within minutes the pain has gone completely, except from my hands, which are bleeding and stinging.

The view from the Trig post at the bare, rocky summit is rather epic, over Holy Island, over the port of Holyhead and over the sea. The sea and the sky are like an artist's pallet, with blue and grey being experimented upon; every shade is represented. The Llyn peninsula is just a vague dark smear. I feel the first big droplets of rain and decide to head down, rapidly but carefully, because I'm sure the café must be open by now. And it is.

* * * * * * * * * * * *

From Holy Island, I cross back onto Anglesey and continue around its coastline. An old couple are sitting in their four-by-four on a traffic island on an A-road, drinking tea from a flask, as though it's the most natural place to stop for a tea break. I wonder if they've broken down and just managed to push their car off the road onto this triangle of grass, but they look quite relaxed and seem to be enjoying the views. Mainly of passing cars.

As there are no other traffic islands available, I opt for the rather lame option of a layby. But it's a nice layby overlooking a beach I know well from childhood. Its Welsh name is Porth Nobla, its English name is "our beach", as in "Mum, Dad, can we go to our beach today?" Schoolfriends had started going abroad on new, cheap package deals to Spanish hotels that hadn't been built yet, when much hilarity would ensue and they still served English food every mealtime. (I've never been on a package holiday, so most of my knowledge about them comes from *Carry On Abroad*.) Regardless of this new foreign trend, we came back to Anglesey as a family most years. This beach distinctly evokes a memory of our first holiday with our new puppy, a golden retriever called Gemma. She experienced sand for the first time and at one point energetically ran into the sea, but stopped dead, eyes wide, staring as the shallow waves lapped over her. She couldn't understand why the water was moving. After that, she was never a fan of water.

The layby is bizarrely littered with playing cards, which is very surreal, like a scene from a 'Sixties TV series: *The Prisoner* or *The Avengers*. As I'm walking along the path around the headland, various cards keep cropping up. It's a bit like having a Tarot reading – by instalments.

I think about paddling, then remember it's bloody freezing. Besides, the beach – as lovely and deserted as it is – stinks of bladderwrack; it's quite overpowering. I walk along the headland path, skirting a recently ploughed field, which is filled with starlings and greylag geese, all pecking happily at the freshly turned earth. I follow the path towards a gaping, manmade doorway cut into the hillside. This is a Neolithic burial chamber, which – following excavations – had a concrete mound erected over it, which was grassed-over, so that from the outside it looks much as it would have done when it was in use. Inside are half a dozen decorated standing stones, carved with zig-zags, spirals and chevrons. It's a Neolithic treasure trove. A tall, slim, elderly lady suddenly appears and hurriedly tells me about the weather, "It's cold and breezy with the possibility of showers later." as though

I'd asked her for a weather forecast, then she turns and strides off briskly.

A jet fighter from RAF Valley, (RAF Y Fali) soars overhead, streaking away across the sky. It's seconds before the sonic boom hits – it's physical, not just aural; I can feel the vibrations in my chest and a thrumming underfoot. The jet arcs around to the airfield and dips below the horizon.

* * * * * * * * * * * *

A short way further along the coast, hidden behind the village of Aberffraw, is a sheltered and secluded rocky bay that currently and inexplicably smells of diesel. Within the bay stands the 13th Century Church of St. Cwyfan's, known as "the Church in the Sea", as it stands on a tiny islet... in the sea. It was built on the end of a peninsula, but the action of the waves eroded the land away, leaving the church cut off at high tide. A set of steep stone steps lead up from the beach. At the top, the restored church is small and basic, with very thick stone walls, whitewashed and gleaming in the flat light. The island is tiny; just grass, with no cover, no shelter, nowhere to go, nowhere to hide. Especially as the church is locked.

A young couple are sitting chatting on a bench on the island, with their lovely whippet-style dog lolloping around looking bored and miserable. She's called Daisy and stares at me in the hope I might rescue her from the monotony.

I say goodbye to the still-chatting couple and Daisy, and carefully descended the slippery steps to the beach. I glance back at the island and see Daisy standing at the top of the steps just staring at me. I continue picking my way between the rocks and stones, over pebbles and seaweed, concentrating on my footsteps. When I look up again, Daisy is a few yards behind me and the island and church are away in the distance. Her mum and dad start calling her, but she's studiously ignoring them, determined to teach them a lesson. She gives me a lost look with her beautiful haunted eyes. I think her mum and dad are either embarrassed or feel betrayed, because they stop calling her and walk off in the opposite direction. I reason with Daisy and try to get her to see sense. She takes what I say on board and with a last lingering look, she trots slowly after them. I watch to make sure she's caught up to them. The next time I glance round they've all gone.

* * * * * * * * * * * *

I drive through the village of Newborough. It was here that we used to stay as a family. Friends of my dad's had bought a property on Anglesey and we used to rent it. I remember the first time my mum mentioned it; she described an idyllic roses-around-the-door country cottage. When we arrived that first time – in the rain, of course – we found a shabby bungalow on a small estate of shabby bungalows. It was such a disappointment. We all got over that disappointment though – although we never warmed to the "Dung Bung" as it was known; it was completely without affection, but we all loved Anglesey, and the Dung Bung enabled us to come for very little cost.

The village of Newborough: the last time I passed this way, it was like Beirut. It looked so rough and run down, but it now looks very respectable. There are several newbuild houses, which have somehow managed to enhance the village and everywhere looks wholesome and less terrifying. Even the Dung Bung, as I pass, looks very respectable. I can't tell which one it is, as it's in a row of identical dung bungs, but they all look nice.

Anglesey seems to be making an effort to be a tourist attraction after decades of coming across as resentful and hostile. It seems to be doing a great job.

* * * * * * * * * * * *

I can't find a suitable place for wild camping in the Newborough area, so I reluctantly book onto one of the very few sites still open at this time of year. It's in the area I want to be in, so that swung it for me. The person running it, I'll call him "Chris" to protect his identity – and because that's what it says on his name badge – is very nice. He looks familiar to me and I eventually realise he reminds me of Richey Edwards from the Manic Street Preachers, who went missing in 1995, then in his late twenties. The resemblance is uncanny.

Chris asks me for some details and taps them into the computer. My name – I get that right. My home address – for some reason I stumble over this. I've only been at this address for four months, but I do know it... and I haven't been travelling so long that I've completely forgotten my previous life. He asks me for the postcode first. The first part I remember, the second part has me flummoxed, which is ludicrous, because it ends with Double D, which is quite memorable. I think Chris thinks I'm making up a fictitious address... not very well. And I don't blame him, because that's what it sounds like to me. I then struggle with the flat number and the house number. I have a system for remembering my phone number, so that miraculously goes off with only a minor stumble. Finally, and with a minimum of hesitation and uncertainty, I'm able to trace the outline of my van registration on the counter. I apologise for my confused mumbling and start to laugh in embarrassment. Chris doesn't laugh. He doesn't laugh at all. He very soberly hands me a long list of site rules and regulations, "dos and don'ts" – mainly don'ts. *Don't do this if that happens.* Do *do that if this happens. Anyone caught doing the other will be asked to leave without a refund.*

Chris asks rather starchily whether I will be dining with them tonight. I didn't know they had a place for dining. Or is he asking me on a date? Either way it's a no, so I politely refuse. He seems a bit affronted. I say goodbye; Chris doesn't reply. I head out to my van and realise he hasn't told me where the toilets or water supply or anything is.

The site's nice and I have a strip of sub-tropical shrubs and plants alongside my pitch, and as a backdrop the dark mountains on the mainland.

I set off for a walk. Heading out along the driveway of the campsite, I pass what appears to be an old outbuilding made of breezeblocks with very narrow slit windows. Inside, there are candles flickering on the tables, there are people eating and it looks warm and cosy, intimate and inviting. It's called *Marram Grass.* I've never had a problem eating alone or going in a pub or cafe on my own, but not on a Friday evening in somewhere where there are candles on the tables and everyone else is at least 50% of a couple having a romantic evening or even just a pre-sex feast. [I later learn that it's run by two brothers and has become one of the most exclusive and fashionable places to eat in Wales. I also check the menu – the pricing is more than I can afford and much more than I can justify for food.] #1

At 3.20pm, it isn't raining. I just need to tell you that. I walk across a nature reserve, Newborough Warren, which is an area of sand dunes and grassland, where rabbits run free and wild ponies graze. It's one of the largest and finest examples of this type of habitat in Europe. Ground nesting birds nest – on the ground – and rare orchids bloom. I don't see any of these flora or fauna, but a noticeboard assures me they're there and that's good enough for me.

During the war, a dummy airfield was set up here to divert enemy bombers away from the genuine target, RAF Valley. Lines of lights were erected to simulate an airstrip, to fool the enemy into dropping their bombs here in this uninhabited area. The HQ for the small team that manned the so called "Q Site" is now on the edge of neighbouring Newborough Forest and is a home for rare bats. The entrance grill is visible still and serves as the access point for the bats.

I follow a footpath into the forest, which is made up largely of evergreen conifers, but with occasional deciduous trees in autumn colours: the yellow of silver birch and the brown of the oaks. Here, the trees are spaced far enough apart to allow sunlight to the forest floor, so ground-covering plants and shrubs can flourish, such as gorse, broom and cotoneaster, unlike tightly-packed, intensive forests, where no sunlight can penetrate, so the ground is just a carpet of dead, dry needles.

The path meanders through the trees, until eventually I emerged through a range of sandhills onto the beach, a wide sandy bay with views to the peaks of the Llyn Peninsula and mainland Wales. The beach is unusually quiet, just a couple of couples with a couple of dogs. The tide is out and the beach feels empty, windswept and alien. A helicopter drones low over the sea. The light is dwindling. Dark clouds are gathering.

At the far end of the bay is Llandwyn Island, only an island at the highest of tides, but still an island with the feeling of an island. Narrow paths snake over the island and around its rocky perimeter. Seabirds settle in their hundreds on the off-shore rocks, most noticeably cormorants, stretching their wings out to dry, in that unmistakable vampiric way.

At the end of the island is the squat lighthouse, now believed to possibly once have been a windmill. It isn't all that impressive as a building, but it occupies a very dramatic setting.

The daylight is fading rapidly. There's just one unbroken blanket of pale grey cloud above and yet again it's trying to rain, so I make my way back along the wide sweep of the bay, then across the Warren. It's hard going through the sandhills, with the ground giving way underfoot; it takes a lot of energy. I suddenly feel really tired and am gasping for a drink.

The last stretch of the walk is along a lane with houses on one side. It's newly dark and the houses have warm lights inside, with their curtains still open. This is Nicky's favourite time of day, because she can stare into other people's homes with impunity. In her absence, I do it for her by proxy. She would be so proud!

* * * * * * * * * * *

I was looking forward to a shower. My first in a few days. The site has signs out boasting "We now have HOT WATER and TWO showers!" I should think they do for what they're charging *in the low season!* It really isn't the best experience for the money and I'm starting to get somewhat irritated by the signs on every surface:

CAUTION – HOT WATER. They boasted about hot water earlier, now they're warning against it! There is also: CHILDREN MUST BE ACCOMPANIED BY ADULTS; SHOWERS ARE FREE TO USE BUT WE ASK THAT YOU LIMIT YOUR SHOWER TO FIVE MINUTES; MAKE SURE THE SHOWER CURTAIN HANGS INSIDE; TO AVOID BLOCKAGE – PLEASE BE CONSIDERATE WITH THE AMOUNT OF TOILET TISSUE YOU USE. There are many, *many* others, but I have to stop somewhere.

* * * * * * * * * * *

The next morning is sunny and beautiful as I drive the last segment of my circumnavigation of Ynys Mon – Anglesey. The scenery is gorgeous; fields dotted with sheep, winding roads, woodlands. I've known Anglesey most of my life and I really love it. It's a place filled with memories. Some of them are even happy ones.

I join the slip-road for the Britannia Bridge. Below the tide is fully in and the water in the Straits is boiling around the various small islands. I cross to the mainland, where the clouds are low over the mountains, but it's still sunny, so I slip my sunglasses on. They're round ones, John Lennon style. Someone said they make me look like Woody Harrelson in *Natural Born Killers*. I've never seen the film myself, but I'm guessing from the title that it's not that nice. So, I look like a killer. A natural born one. But a killer nevertheless. Not something you necessarily want on your CV.

With a hop and a skip, I'm back in mainland Wales.

Hwyl fawr, Ynys Môn!

* * * * * * * * * * * *

If Brendan was with me...

Some time later, when I first took Brendan to a beach, he also reacted the same as our family dog, Gemma. He ran into the water and then froze. When it moved he did an about-turn and ran away, never to return into its evil clutches. I've taken Brendan to Anglesey many times; apart from staying at home, it's probably his favourite place.

NOTES

#1: I passed Marram Grass recently. It was in darkness and appeared derelict. Turns out it closed permanently in 2021 due to the Covid pandemic.

ABOVE: Trwyn Du lighthouse, Penmon Point.

ABOVE: South Stack at sunet.

CHAPTER 7: PENRHYN LLYN

In which I am not a number – I am a free man. I see castles and coves and am highly "choughed".

Caernarfon is a beautiful, historic city, ("the townies", "pigshit scum", "the place is full of psychopaths") despite the townies, pigshit scum and psychopaths – of which I can't see any trace. The Romans built a fort here in AD80, possibly to keep the townies, pigshit scum and psychopaths in check. They liked it so much they stayed for the next three centuries, until the end of the Roman occupation in AD382, when they donned their sandals and, if I know those Romans, they marched in a straight line all the way back to Rome. Caernarfon is situated on the Menai Straits and faces the coast of Anglesey. The Romans waded across the Straits to finish off the Druids once and for all. Everyone needs a hobby.

I walk from the car park into the centre of the old town, passing a gang of supermarket staff who are huddled together on a smoking break. They're all staring at me as I approach and I realise I'm wearing my "racist" hoodie; it has a Union Jack emblazoned on the front, which in Wales I always worry might be taken as some sort of anti-nationalist slur against anyone who wants autonomy from the English – and it isn't. I button up my jacket to hide my secret shame. (It doesn't button up as well as it used to – it has become much tighter fitting.) I then realise, the jacket is an ex-army camouflage-type thing –

it was dyed black when I bought it in Camden Market on a punk stall, but with every wash it loses more of its adopted colour, so people could possibly see me as a militarised fascist as well as a would-be subjugator of the non-English British peoples. Modern life can be very complicated and stressful.

A while back, in the late 11th century, a real-life subjugator called William – "the Conqueror" to his friends – failed to conquer the Welsh, but in the 13th Century Edward I succeeded – he was probably wearing a Union Jack hoodie at the time. He set about building Caernarfon Castle, considered by many to be the best castle built by the English in Wales. It is remarkably intact and well-preserved. It dominates the old town, with its size, its scale, the stark angles and its overall design. It is thought the distinctive polygonal towers and coloured stonework were intended to emulate the walls of Constantinople; having never been to Istanbul, not Constantinople, I can't vouch for this, but it is certainly impressive. You can't help feeling a sense of awe when looking at the castle. It's magnificent.

Today, Caernarfon is very much a tourist town, with the castle, marina, old town, the Roman fort and the new kid on the block, Doc Fictoria (Victoria Dock), which was opened in 2008. Like many towns, Caernarfon's docks have been regenerated and given a new lease of life. There are residential apartments, but also hotels and restaurants. The only problem for me, is that it's all newbuild and is strangely soulless. Perhaps it hasn't taken off yet. There doesn't seem enough here to make it feel busy, bustling and vibrant. I know it's a grey day out of season, but on this occasion, I'm one of only three people wandering around the dock.

The marina is filled with very expensive boats, any one of which I'd happily accept as a gift. There is a wide promenade along the Menai Straits, giving views across to Anglesey, which looks to be a green and pleasant land. The ideally located *Anglesey* pub, is situated on the Straits promenade. It would be tempting to sit outside and look at the amazing view with the constant cry of the gulls drifting across the sand banks and echoing from the high castle walls; it would be tempting in summer, but not today.

Apparently, there are more Welsh speakers in Caernarfon than anywhere else, and as if to prove a point, every single person that passes me on the sea front is speaking Welsh.

The old part of town fits snugly into the town walls. The high towers of the castle itself come back into view, towering above the river and harbour. Close-up its sheer height makes it look impregnable.

I spot some public toilets, which are free. I feel I ought not to pass up this opportunity, so I go in for a free wee. Inside, I'm surprised to see a "sharps bin", for used hypodermics, only it's been doctored and now reads: "harps only", which seems so quaintly Welsh.

The market square is known locally as the "maes" – the place – and is a multi-user space for pedestrians and motors, which causes some confusion and is not popular with the townsfolk. It's a wide market square surrounded by little shops and overlooked by the towering castle. It's a nice place to sit or dodge traffic. In the maes is a statue of

David Lloyd George, who had been MP for the area. It was erected in 1921 when he had become Prime Minister.

The old part of town, within the walls, is criss-crossed with quirky little back streets of colourful painted shops, including a haberdasher, alongside cafes and pubs. Outside one fine old pub, a poor delivery man has dropped a crate of bottled beers. Some of the bottles have smashed and a foaming slick of froth is spreading out across the cobbles. Quite a crowd is gathering, staring down in dismay at the increasing puddle, as though mourning the loss of a fallen comrade. Rivulets of dark ale weave between the cobbles in a shape not unlike a London Tube map.

I return to the van, again passing the smokers, who are still in a huddle drawing desperately on their cigarettes and staring accusingly. I wonder if any work ever gets done at that supermarket. The first thing I do on entering Eagle One is change out of my offensive hoodie, swapping it for a plain one - one which is less likely to cause a bar brawl.

On leaving Caernarfon, there are views ahead of the dramatic mountains along the Llyn Peninsula. The nearest slopes are green and farmed, dissected by drystone walls and hedgerows, but further away they become less green, less farmed, darker, covered with bracken, gorse and heather, then barren and craggy. They become quarried, cut into steps where they had been worked years ago. The tops are all shrouded in cloud. On the seaward side, they plummet in a sheer drop into the ocean.

I leave the A-road and follow a B-road steeply uphill. On my right a dark, ragged slope is rising into nothingness, with several footpaths leading up into the water vapour. On a better day, I plan to climb this mountain, because at the top is *Tre'r Ceiri*, "the town of giants", an Iron Age hillfort from around 200 BC, which was occupied for several hundred years. It is remarkably well-preserved and has stone walls up to four metres high in places. Within its perimeter ramparts are the impressive remains of around 150 stone houses. The setting, the location and the fact you've had to put in so much effort to get there make this a magnificent and rewarding place. I've tried to get there several times, but only succeeded once, due to changes in weather and conditions. Yet again, it isn't for today, due to time.

I reach my destination as the light is fading: a car park at the foot of the main peak of Yr Eifl, meaning "the forks", as the three peaks that make up this micro-range supposedly resemble the prongs of a fork. (They really don't!) There is one other car in the car park. The car is empty. A layer of low cloud blocks the mountain at the half way point, like a painting that's been partially erased. As the evening descends, the white, ether-like mist seems to be rolling down the mountainside, an eerie, obliterating white cloud. I watch as it descends and the horizon grows lower. It's quite unnerving.

I see the last of the light fade and the low cloud smothers the land. The very occasional full beams of approaching vehicles send searchlights skating across the empty landscape. I watch until it's completely dark, listening to the sounds, the breeze, not much else, enjoying the atmosphere, enjoying being there.

By 7pm, everything outside the windows has completely gone. There is nothing at all. It's really foggy and very spooky. I step outside. There is very little wind down here, but I can hear it up in the darkness, in the mist, presumably blasting through the rocks on the Rivals. There's no trace of any light at all; I can make out the difference between the dark grey of the sky and the black of the land, but nothing else. It's very rarely completely dark, even at night, but the cloud layer is too thick to allow any moonlight through or any trace of the stars.

At 8pm, I hear the crunching of tyres on gravel and look outside, hoping another camper van is pulling in to stay the night. I can't see any vehicle, no headlights or tail lights; they have either gone or are lost in the fog. As I'm typing up my notes, I think I can hear the slamming of a car door. I then think I can hear rhythmic footsteps, but it turns out to be just the ticking of my clock. I don't think I've ever been anywhere so utterly dark before. I suddenly wish I was on a site. It's quite chilly, but not too bad considering I haven't got any heating on at all. I have turned the diesel heater off to save fuel and am sitting up in bed for warmth. At home, Nicky is teaching her dancing class, as she does every Tuesday evening. She seems a long way away.

At 8.30, I definitely hear another car. This time I can see it. It has reversed into a parking space across the car park. It isn't a camper van hoping to spend the night here. A car could only be here in these dark, impenetrable conditions for one reason.

I fall asleep, but at 2.30am I wake up again. My pillow is soaked with condensed breath. Or dribble. It's very cold and is raining. I lie awake, listening to the pleasing sound as the raindrops hit the roof. I'm not thinking about anything to do with the future, which is good; again I'm existing totally in the present, which is great. I listen to the rhythmic pattering and eventually fall asleep again.

I'm awoken by my alarm at 7am. The rain has stopped. It's cloudy with banks of mist trapped in the hollows of the landscape, but I can see the rocky top of the mountain now.

I really want a strong coffee and I know the nearby Welsh Language Centre has a nice café with views out to sea. The road leads very steeply downhill with several hairpin bends – if your brakes were failing you wouldn't want to be there. And you wouldn't be for long. At the bottom is Nant Gwrtheyrn, which means "Vortigern's Valley". Vortigern was possibly a 5th-century warlord, possibly known as King of the Britons who possibly fled to Wales. It's possible he was buried in Wales, in Dyfed or the Llyn Peninsula. A barrow once existed in this area known as Vortigern's Grave. He may possibly have been buried there... or he may possibly not. According to some scholars, he may not ever have existed at all.

With this in mind, I drive down the steep winding lane to Nant. Possible dead kings aside, it's a lovely, restored community. It's hard to believe this was ever a derelict former mining village called Porth y Nant, which was abandoned when quarrying stopped during World War II, though the evidence is still apparent. On the surrounding steep hills are old buildings with gaping, empty windows and collapsing roofs, being gradually absorbed into the landscape.

The café isn't open. All the windows have blinds down, but there are lights on inside and I can see movement in the kitchens. The website says it opens at 8.30 and it's now gone 9am. There's no sign on the door explaining the unscheduled closure, which really annoys me. I knock on the door, but no one answers. I leave Nant without a coffee and continue around the coast of the Llyn Peninsula.

I drive through Porth Nefyn which has a lovely beach and harbour. The area has had some seismic activity in the past; a tremor recorded in 1940 and in 1984 an earthquake measuring 5.4 on the Richter scale. This was one of the strongest tremors recorded in Britain in recent times; it caused some minor damage, but not enough to base a disaster movie on it.

A short way further on, is Porthdinllaen, which is one of my very favourite places in the world. It's a tiny hamlet in a sheltered and secluded cove. Part of its charm is that it isn't accessible (by the general public) by road – you have to walk along the beach, a stroll of some twenty minutes. This makes it feel more remote than it actually is. It's a compact jumble of different architectural styles, weather-boarding, whitewashed stone, huddled together right on the beach. It has been owned by the National Trust since 1994. Standing out amongst the white buildings is one red house, the inn, the *Ty Coch* – literally the Red House – famous as one of the top ten beach pubs in the world. It has a no chip policy. It doesn't serve chips. At all. Ever!

It's a joy to sit there eating a baked potato with three bean chilli and listen to the indignation and trauma of other patrons as they read the menu and learn they can't have chips.

In the sunshine, this secluded bay looks like a gorgeous Aegean scene, with soft, white sand and the sea lapping gently: a sea of shimmering turquoise or aquamarine or azure... and other colours that are names of paint, when blue just won't do. At other times, with a biting Siberian breeze, it looks very Scottish, remote and eerie. Indeed, in September 2004 it posed as a Scottish fishing village for the Demi Moore unthriller *Half Light*. Regardless of which persona it adopts, this bay is one of the most beautiful places in Wales. At a glance it looks very similar to Portmeirion, except – despite its eclectic nature, it fits together neatly and none of the architecture jars. If I could choose to live anywhere in Britain, I would almost certainly choose Porthdinllaen. The only problem would be its popularity; you'd constantly get people like me peering in your windows, admiring your chimneypots and photographing your gables. And nobody wants that.

Today, midweek and out of season, the pub – the hub of the village – is closed and stands in darkness. With most of the cottages now being holiday lets, the village is deserted, like a post-apocalyptic ghost town, but still the prettiest post-apocalyptic ghost town I've ever seen.

* * * * * * * * * *

Driving along, I realise I'm not happy. I find I'm starting to think about which direction I should travel in. In life, I mean, not on the roads. I stop at temporary traffic lights.

I really do, this isn't a metaphor; there are roadworks. I have my elbows on the steering wheel, idly watching the workmen in hard hats and hi-viz jackets while I wait for the lights to change. They have a hard job, as well as hard hats; they're out in the cold and the rain, but also the blazing sunshine – when we have it. On the plus side they work in a team, a unit, there is camaraderie, a laugh and a joke. It's not something I think I need, but it's very healthy and very normal, and I suppose I miss it in many ways. In some ways. Sometimes. But not all the time. Probably hardly ever. I've kept in touch with friends from work, but it isn't the same as being colleagues working towards the same goals. Not that I think we ever worked towards the same goals. I often felt I was moving in the opposite direction. On my own. I grew to hate work. But I miss it. And every day I'm thankful I'm no longer there.

The lights change: amber and then green and I drive on, passing the workmen, feeling a bit jealous, which is ludicrous, because in all likelihood any one of them would gladly swap places with me as I sail nobly along in Eagle One.

* * * * * * * * * *

I park in a National Trust car park – again there's only one other car there – and walk along an undulating clifftop path. The sea crashes on the dark rocks and the clouds roll by, which suits my mood. I'm still feeling reflective and subdued and it's gone on long enough. I'm completely alone on the clifftop. It's time for *International Rescue*. If you're feeling blue, I'll tell you what to do: hum the theme to Thunderbirds, it'll cheer you through and through. And it did. You cannot trudge along dub-dub-a-dumming

"Thunderbirds" and not start to laugh. And I *do* laugh... but possibly in a way that if anyone had overheard they may well have called for back-up.

Feeling a lot happier, I follow the path as it descends into a beautiful bay of wall-to-wall sand, backed by steep grassy cliffs. Porth Oer is its Welsh name; Whistling Sands is its English name, because the sand makes squeaking noises when you stand on it, due to the shape of the crystals and the weight of the foot. There are only two beaches in the whole of Europe where this happens. I step onto the sand with a mounting sense of trepidation. My feet make contact with the myriad grains and... I can now reveal that today, Porth Oer is a whistle-free zone. Perhaps it's too wet or cold, whatever the reason, there is no whistle. I try higher up the beach where the sand is drier and powdery-white. Still nothing. Its whistle is depleted, its melody is no more.

Walking back along the cliff top path, I think I've spotted a chough (the bird), but I'm wrong. I'm always wrong. I've never seen a chough. The Llyn Peninsula is famous for them; the bird features on the logo, with its distinctive red legs and beak. There are supposed to be 60 breeding pairs here. I've often seen black birds and excitedly looked closer, only to see they have the black beak of a raven or other corvid, rather than the distinctive red of a chough.

I have a brew, watch the storm clouds gathering then leave Porth Oer to get its whistle repaired.

Although it isn't far as the chough flies, the journey to the tip of the peninsula takes some time, due to the single track, constantly winding lanes. The further along the peninsula I drive, the fewer houses there are and they're set in hamlets rather than villages. They're stone built and whitewashed. As it's more exposed here, all buildings seem to crouch low, hugging the earth, as though an indigenous part of the landscape.

The road is a dead-end; it terminates at Mynydd Mawr, which means "big mountain". It's neither big nor a mountain, but let's not quibble. It's a very attractive small hill, ideally placed for viewing Bardsey Island, which is, and I quote "the fourth largest offshore island in Wales". (If an island isn't "offshore" isn't it called the "mainland"?) Anyway, it's known as the "Island of 20,000 Saints" and it lies just under two miles off the tip of the Llyn Peninsula. It has its very own lighthouse, an unusual square tower with red and white banding, which is clearly visible from here.

Bardsey is a mile long and has several occupants. It has on it a big hill, more worthy of being called Mynydd Mawr than Mynydd Mawr is, because it is indeed *one great big hill*; it dwarfs the lighthouse. The rest of the island is flat. According to one legend, it is the burial place of King Arthur. Half the country is claiming an Arthur connection, including my sock drawer: his *real* resting place.

I park in the small car park at the summit of Mynydd Mawr. It was used during the Second World War as an air raid look-out station. Concrete steps lead down to the foundations of several military ruins. The cliffs are a popular nesting site for a whole posse of birds: choughs, peregrine falcons, kestrels, puffins and guillemots. I'm pretty sure I spot a pair of choughs, but they're too far away to see the colour of their beaks. Choughs are monogamous; they tend to pair for life and remain loyal to their cliff crevice breeding sites. They have red beaks and legs. They are a member of the corvid or crow family, as are jackdaws. Their call is – apparently – a "loud ringing chee-ow". I couldn't swear that's the sound this pair are making, but they have a loud and distinctive cry and I am positively chalking them up as choughs.

There's rain in the strong wind and dark clouds above, but there's a bright band of light on the horizon. Bardsey Island looks surreal, super-imposed. It looks mythical and magical and it's really starting to look an appropriately ethereal burial place for King Arthur. An inky blackness is spreading over the sea.

I had been planning to stay overnight at the car park on Mynydd Mawr, but I've got no mobile signal at all – which I'm not keen on when parked in a strange place – and it is incredibly windy. So, I set off along the narrow lanes towards Aberdaron, a former fishing village, shipbuilding, mining and quarrying centre. It was the last port of call for pilgrims heading over to the monastery on Bardsey Island. Today, it's primarily a holiday resort, sometimes referred to as the "Land's End of Wales". It's small, whitewashed, pleasant enough, but nothing like Land's End.

After a complicated drive and a few arguments with SatNav Sally, I arrive in Abersoch ("Dog muck", "it turns in to a ghost town", "drunken farmers", "the weather"), yet another former fishing village and sea port that has turned its hand to tourism and specialises in watersports. It has become quite exclusive these days, with modern bars and bistros and designer clothes shops. Abersoch was named as one of the best places to live in Wales in 2017.

The roads suddenly become busier, with people heading home from work and in a great hurry to do so. While Abersoch could be called pretentious, the same couldn't be said for Pwllheli. ("Desperately provincial", "exists only for the locals", "stunning ignorance and apathy", "over zealous nationalism"). It has coloured lights strung above its main streets and the pubs all seem to be flashing inside with the chaotic flickering of fruit machines. Pwllheli is the main market town of the Llyn Peninsula, where 81% are Welsh-speakers. It's a town where people live, work and shop, not really a tourist town. The Welsh independent party, Plaid Cymru, was founded here.

The market is finishing for the day and the stalls are being cleared away. Manual workers in hard hats are returning home with takeaways in white plastic bags. I follow suit and order a Chinese takeaway, despite me not having a hard hat. I'm served by two very bored non-Chinese people, who seem annoyed that I've interrupted their conversation.

With my bag of hot food, I drive around the darkened marina looking for somewhere to park and eat my meal. It's a largely regenerated area; I love water and I love boats, but this seems a bit bleak, like an industrial estate with some yachts hastily chucked into it. It's very, very dark and a bit soulless. I stop in a large boat club car park to eat my Chinese. I'm really looking forward to it, but it tastes how Chinese tastes if you've made it at home, using microwave rice and a cook-in sauce from the pound shop.

I eat it because I'm hungry and I've paid for it, but it's very poor. If I'm paying for food I really want it to be better than I can make myself.

I follow directions from a website to a place where overnight wild camping is permitted. I eventually find it: a spit of land jutting out into the sea, close to the entrance to Pwllheli harbour. There are buoys flashing green and red. Across the sea, I can see the lights of mid-Wales. It feels very isolated and very spooky. I can hear the sea on three sides, but not actually see it.

I'm too tired to search for another place; this is the fourth location I've checked out tonight; the others had all proved unsuitable for one reason or another. This has been highly recommended by a website, but they warn to be careful where you park due to the rising tide. I check the ground as best I can, though it's difficult in the dark, even with a torch I can't be sure whether the ground is damp or sea-wet. I park where I think it's probably safest, but I feel really agitated, unsettled and vulnerable.

It starts to rain at 9pm and the wind is picking up. No other vans come to join me. I watch an episode of *Northern Exposure,* a light-hearted comedy-drama set in Alaska. I like the feeling of isolation and remoteness of the setting, which connects partly with my love of lighthouses and islands. Within half an hour, I have completely relaxed and it feels like home. I abandon any fear of the incoming tide and of being murdered in the night and I settle down for the evening.

* * * * * * * * * *

I wake up at 6am. Outside it's still dark and blowing a gale. I'm still on dry land as far as I can tell. For the moment. But it's half an hour to high tide.

When dawn breaks, I look out and see a van has arrived from the sewage pollution agency. That can't be good. The car park is a mass of flooded potholes. I had assumed they were filled with rainwater. I *hoped* they were filled with rainwater. A man with a tiny dog walks past and his dog abruptly stops and creates a little bit more of a sewage problem.

I take my first proper look at my surroundings in daylight: a spit of land with a huge bank of shale on one side, stone sea defences on all other sides. This spit, the shale bank and the roughly hewn rocks are all here to create a barrier between the sea and the marina. I'm facing seawards. There are occasional shrubs and clumps of marram grass, blowing in a strong gale. The sea looks grey and angry. It's really quite a nice, if barren spot. I have a cup of tea – it's what I do when I find myself in a nice, if barren spot. I sit with my book on my lap, but don't read it, I don't take my eyes off the sea, its surging movements and the occasional spasm of rain that pelts the windscreen.

This is what it's all about: seeing the different scenery and experiencing places and what they've got to offer. *This* is what I want to see on my trip: Britain being Britain, regardless of what weather it may throw at me.

At 11.30, I leave the van for the first time. It's cold and breezy, but it's stopped raining and is now suddenly, bizarrely, gloriously sunny. I can see the edge of Llyn and then the rest of the mainland stretching away. The sky is a deep blue with tufty white clouds.

I drive away, having enjoyed my rather lazy morning. I pass the gates of what was once Butlins at Pwllheli. (It's still open as a holiday camp, but no longer a Butlins.) It was here that comedy scriptwriter, Jimmy Perry, had worked as a Red Coat. He was very much a man inspired by his own experiences; *Dad's Army* came about because as a teenager Perry volunteered for the Home Guards. His army years were spent in Burma, where he joined the concert party, resulting in *It Ain't Half Hot Mum*. His experiences at Butlins, of course, would provide the basis for *Hi-Di-Hi*.

I drive through Llanystumdwy, which has strong connections with David Lloyd George, whose statue I had seen in Caernarfon in the market square. Lloyd George was one of the most popular British prime ministers, and his popularity is enduring, as he's still voted one of the top British PMs of all time. He was born in Manchester, though both his parents were Welsh.

Lloyd George was prime minister during World War I, but is better remembered today for his introduction of the Welfare State, including old age pensions. Lloyd George is buried close to the river in a quiet spot on the edge of the village. He requested no traditional gravestone, so instead a boulder marks his resting place. The later addition of an ornamental enclosure and gate, designed by Portmeirion's Clough Williams-Ellis, has made it into a very pleasant, shady shrine.

* * * * * * * * * *

I haven't always had the best relationship with Criccieth. In the past, it's always seemed somewhere people were very fond of, but every time I've visited I've been disappointed. The last time I couldn't actually find anything; it just seemed to be houses without an actual centre or anywhere to aim for. This time, I am determined to find the *real* Criccieth.

I manage to park on the esplanade, wedged between three or four school minibuses, with dozens of the young inhabitants swarming all over the beach. Criccieth has two beaches, with the castle mound separating them. Today, the spectacular castle dominates the town and the landscape for miles around and is in an excellent state of repair. A slow-motion seagull glides effortlessly over the turrets, ascending into the blue.

I stroll around and pass a Cadwalanders, a Welsh chain of coffee shops. I've never seen it here before. The thing that catches my attention is, at the very back, there are wide windows looking out over the bay. A large Americano later, I'm sitting in the prime position, eyes on the gentle white-edged waves with the sun beating down through the glass roof and I'm on a gentle simmer. Bad Christmas carols are blaring out. It's way too early! Christmas is two months away! I'm very much a "keep Christmas-in-December" sort of chap.

I leave the café and step outside into high summer weather. It's hard to believe conditions were so bad earlier in the morning. Two young girls are walking towards me holding hands, not as female friends might – no, their manner says: "Yeah, we're lesbians – get over it!" I disappoint them by not reacting at all. I live in Manchester – we've covered lesbianism and more besides.

I pass the Castle entrance. It's only a fiver to go in and although I'm sure it's worth every non-European penny... and I 'm very tempted... wherever possible I'm trying to find alternatives to the general tourist attractions, so I turn down a narrow side street and look through people's windows instead. The cottages are small, but very attractive, built on a steep hill. Most are neatly painted in bright seaside colours and have slate signs bearing the cottage names. *Pentre isaf, Ty Newydd, Ynysgain, Affalon* and the less imaginatively named *Three*.

With that activity under my belt, I return to Eagle One on the esplanade and sit inside having my lunch. People passing by on the pavement keep staring in and invariably making comments to each other, probably because my food is healthy and colourful and not usual camping food out of a tin. I'm on my current favourite: mashed avocado on lightly toasted sourdough bread with an accompanying salad, including orange rapture tomatoes – which are orange. And totally rapturous. I reason that if I have a healthy lunch I can eat chocolate digestives all afternoon with a clear conscience.

* * * * * * * * * *

Porthmadog ("The Weather when it's horrible' it's really really horrible. The house prices..getting just too silly The Trains and the associated fannies" (sic), "Bigoted self opinionated locals who think the world owes them a living") (sic) is another of those places that isn't so much a holiday town, as a town in a holiday area. It wouldn't win any awards for its aesthetics, but it can provide you with almost everything you need.

With that in mind, I stop briefly at a supermarket for food shopping. In the car park, a teenage boy passes me, energetically leap-frogging over a series of waist-high metal posts. He's alone, so he isn't showing off, he isn't trying to impress anyone, it's just for fun, because he can. I really admire his child-like enthusiasm. He clears the first two posts admirably, with some athletic prowess, but unfortunately comes a cropper on the third, misjudging or mistiming and slamming his crotch into the top of it. Instinctively, I wince on his behalf. In true British fashion, he carries on walking, trying to pretend nothing has happened, but he's limping quite badly and seems unable to catch his breath properly. He'll probably think twice before he tries that again.

With a van full of food, I drive on through Porthmadog, which came into being when William Maddocks, after whom the town is named, constructed a sea wall to reclaim land for agricultural use. This wall, called the Cob, carries the tracks of the Ffestiniog Railway. Originally, the little train brought slate down from the mountains of Blaenau to be exported via the harbour at Porthmadog.

There are now beautiful views of the mountains, drenched in sunlight, looking dry and hazy. It makes me frustrated to be driving and not out enjoying the landscape. On the plus-side, I traverse two toll bridges, neither of which are manned today, so I pocket the thirty-five pence I've saved and promise myself I'll invest it wisely. In cake.

Over the estuary, shimmering in the sunshine, I can see the white buildings of the seaward side of Portmeirion, the fantasy village created by "errant architect", Sir Clough Williams-Ellis. It was here that *The Prisoner* was famously filmed in the 'Sixties. *The Prisoner* was the brainchild of genius or maverick actor, director, writer, thinker and everyman, Patrick McGoohan; it is considered to be either the most influential and ground-breaking TV series of all time or a pile of utter tripe. I LOVE *The Prisoner*, but I love the concept more than the reality. I love what *The Prisoner* could have been rather than what it is. It has certainly been inspirational and has inspired writers, artists and film-makers for generations. It has inspired me. #1

I drive on through the sunshine, leaving Portmeirion and the Lynn Peninsula behind, heading for mid-Wales.

Be seeing you.

* * * * * * * * * * *

If Brendan was with me...

A few years later I actually got to *Tre'r Ceiri* with Brendan. I was amazed he made it, because it's quite a climb, but he raced up, then went to sleep in one of the ruins at the top. I was so proud of him. For his mountaineering skills, I mean - not the fact that he went to sleep somewhere, because he does that all the time.

Nicky and I used to stay at Portmeirion several times a year. We went with our dog, Cindy, and stayed in various self-catering cottages within the village itself. Over the years Portmeirion has sadly reduced its dog-friendly accommodation, so Brendan has never been. But he's not too bothered, because he's been to our local field and that's ticked all his boxes.

ABOVE: Can you spot the imposter?
One of these beach huts is undercover – badly.

ABOVE: At the foot of Garn Ganol

ABOVE: Bardsey Island, the "Island of 20,000 Saints"

ABOVE: "I am not a number!" Home of the Prisoner, Portmeirion.

NOTES

#1. My play *The Long Goodbye* was in part an homage to *The Prisoner*.

CHAPTER 8: TWIN ESTUARIES

In which I visit the "village of the damned". I learn about the last Welsh Prince of Wales and I *don't* hear the bells of Aberdovey.

The road to Harlech is lined with overhanging trees in autumn colours, but I'm not really able to appreciate the autumnal spectacle. The road is narrow and winds tightly. Despite their vehicles having steering wheels, oncoming drivers don't always use them to stick to their side of the road when coming around the bends, so it's quite a stressful and hazardous journey.

I'm thankful when I arrive in Harlech. In the middle of the village, a woman steps into the road right in front of me. Eagle One has a diesel engine and isn't a stealth craft by any means, so she should have heard my approach. Thanks to my anticipation, sensible speed and quick reactions I don't hit her. I don't think she even knows I'm there or that she's narrowly avoided certain death. Or at least a mild graze. (I regret not giving her a severe horning.)

Harlech is the most alive I've ever seen it; however, it's still sleepy and appears largely unpopulated. The car park only has five cars in it. It isn't in any way unpleasant, but it never seems to be open and there's nothing here except the castle, but it's a fine castle in a commanding location, visible for miles around. It looks especially magnificent in the sunshine.

Harlech, of course, is famous for its men. In the song. *Men of Harlech*. The town is synonymous with singing; it's seemingly a place where the chaps get together in the evenings and belt out a few tunes, unhindered by their womenfolk. I refer, of course, to Welsh male voice choirs. (I've just Googled and found astoundingly, there isn't actually a local male voice choir called *The Men of Harlech*. A missed opportunity, surely.)

If I was making a TV documentary, I would have to check out a local male voice choir and join in, which would result in much embarrassed hilarity. Fortunately, I'm not, so I don't and it won't. I drive off instead. Thanks to several moments of grinding gears, this causes ample embarrassment and hilarity anyway, for me and the onlookers in the car park respectively. The meshing is going on second gear; accordingly, I try my best to avoid second gear, but that isn't always an option.

It's only a short drive to my site for the night, Shell Island. In my childhood, Welsh tourist leaflets used to run the catchy strap-line "Shell Island – famous for shells". Even in single figures, I thought this took lack of imagination to extremes. It's so naff it's hilarious!

The island – along with its celebrity shells – is connected to the mainland by a tidal causeway and is only cut off at high tide. It's a beautiful spot with amazing views of the sea, the bay and the mountains. Apart from the golden sandy beaches, the main attraction of Shell Island is that it's a campsite; a colossal campsite; acres of grass and sand dunes – you just pitch where you like. It's a bit of a free-for-all in that respect. There are no marked pitches, no boundaries, no reservations. I've never been to Glastonbury, but I imagine it's a bit like that, but with more flip-flops and less sewage overflow.

It is largely populated by huge family groups, with a dozen tents of varying sizes, all connected and contained by miles of windbreaks. There are whole cities of canvas and multi-generational clans seem to come on holiday together. By the look of it I'm the only person who's come as a person, singular, untogether and alone. Caravans aren't allowed on the island and there are very few vans, it's mainly tents. Wherever you go, every corner you turn, every sand dune you climb, you're confronted by a tented hamlet. It's very reasonably priced, because it is a stunning location with great views across Tremadog Bay to the jagged outline of the Llyn Peninsula and inland towards the dark, foreboding mountains of southern Snowdonia. My own cynical view is that it is a lovely campsite ruined by campers.

I pull up in one of the few spaces I can find, but it's very exposed and I don't like it. It all feels very public and that really isn't for me. I go for a walk to the beach, which is wide and sandy. I paddle, but not for long – it's absolutely freezing. I can't find any impressive shells, only razors, which are fairly common. Famous for shells? More like famous for shell suits.

Many of the tents have tall flags flying; I now realise it is most likely to help you locate your dwelling. Because it isn't regimented, it's easy to get lost. Despite having a map, I can't find my van for a full hour.

In the early evening, I have a walk to the northern-most tip of the island where there's a little harbour, a sheltered bay filled with boats and yachts. Despite it getting quite cold, breezy and the sun being hidden behind a dark bank of cloud, some boys are swimming in the sea – in an area designated "unsafe for swimming". They have an adult with them, overseeing from the beach, so at least if they are swept out to sea and drowned, he would know about it.

I return to Eagle One and set about preparing my tea. The gas seems to run out suddenly, unexpectedly, so I have cold soup and bread. I've had better meals.

After dark, I walk to the shower block. The whole island is aglow. Most tents have flashing lights, fairy lights or strings of lanterns; it's like some nylon Vegas. Many also have fires, fire pits, log burners, nuclear reactors or barbecues. Even in the dark I can see the night air is grey with a fug of smoke and it smells of lighter fluid.

I spend the evening in my van, of course, alone – of course. I've got no gas and no electric hook-up, so I can't make a cup of tea and I can't watch anything. I try reading, but for some of the time I just sit in the darkness feeling very incongruous. I haven't brought a hoard of children and I'm completely on my own. I haven't seen anyone else on their own, so I feel like an outsider and a misfit, intruding in this child-friendly world where I don't belong. This is clearly a great place for a family get-together and perfect for children, but it's not really suitable for me.

At 9.30pm there is an exodus of families from the on-site bar, waves of tottering pilgrims heading back to their canvas communities. There is laughter and merriment and music, but at ten o'clock sharp it goes silent, as per the rules and I don't hear another sound.

I sleep very well and awake to a grey and miserable morning, but the sun soon comes up. People are driving to the toilets, even though there are small toilet blocks at very regular intervals. I've never seen anything like it.

I pack up and leave, but manage to buy a new gas bottle on the way out from the camp shop. Well done Shell Island! At the first opportunity I'll be pulling over to make a brew and trying out my new gas!

* * * * * * * * * *

I continue ever-southwards, ever anti-clockwise, swinging through small hamlets and a pleasantly green landscape. I pass through the village of Morfa Dyffryn, which has a nudist beach – apparently. Famous all over the world – apparently! I've been here before, but never seen even a hint of nakedness! I feel a little bit short-changed. Short-changed by people with nowhere to keep their change.

I drive through Barmouth in the approaching darkness. ("Bloody chav tourists", "small town mentality", "summer and sea gulls") I call into a Co-op, where I see a middle-aged man laughing at vegetables. I don't know whether they're in rude shapes or if he just finds vegetables hilarious.

Barmouth became popular as a Victorian holiday destination, hence its Anglicised name. Its Welsh name is Abermaw – "aber" meaning mouth of the river and "maw" from the river Mawddach. The Welsh are very consistent when it comes to their place names.

I park on the esplanade. The sun is setting over the sea and it's suddenly bitterly cold. The people walking their dogs along the prom are wearing hats and gloves and it feels very wintery. I drive up and down looking for a suitable place to stop for the night, but there are NO OVERNIGHT PARKING signs everywhere. So, I reluctantly leave Barmouth along the estuary road, where there's a piece of nationalist graffiti sprayed onto a wide rockface: FREE WALES. I cross the river via a lovely old wooden toll bridge, where a nice chap relieves me of a pound coin.

"Gone cold." he says, which is true. "Was quite mild 'til this afternoon." Also true.

So, it isn't just the English who are obsessed with talking about the weather – it must be the British in general. I bid him farewell and tell him to stay warm.

"I'm going to try to!" he chuckles.

I park in a nearby car park, overlooking the river. There's an honesty box if you stay overnight. There's a pub a short walk away, so I look up the menu on the internet. The website comes up with a block and asks me: "Are you REALLY over 18?" I find this bizarre. It's the REALLY that gets me, because if I was a child hacking into a pornographic menu I would hardly be honest at that point and tick "No". Anyway, being legally over 18, I access the site, only there isn't a menu. They're updating it. Does that mean they aren't serving food then? No, of course it doesn't, so they could put a temporary menu on, but they don't. I feel quite annoyed and open a tin of beans instead. Punishing them for their inefficiency is the only way they'll learn!

I feel a bit cheated; I've done so much driving today – and driving while the sun was shining, which seems such a waste. I had been too concerned with trying to find a campsite, so I could recharge everything and have a shower and a peaceful night somewhere I felt safe. Sunshine is a precious commodity in Britain and it should be enjoyed and used wisely. I feel like I've not made the most of the day.

At 9pm, a car drives in and parks very close to my van. I can't see who's inside, but the interior is lit up by a red light. It all seems quite suspicious. I close my curtains tighter. Eventually I hear the car drive off.

There are lots of stars visible, as there is very little light pollution, but I don't want to get out and look at them. I'm enjoying the warmth and comfort inside Eagle One too much.

Quite a few more cars come and go throughout the evening, but I feel secure and contented here, with the nocturnal animal calls over the estuary and a cloudless sky full of stars.

* * * * * * * * * *

When I open the curtains at dawn, a car suddenly drives off at speed. I don't know whether it had been there all night – which seems unlikely – whether it was up to no good, or whether it was just a coincidence. There is a damp, cloying greyness in the air. Mist hangs in heavy strands over the chocolate brown of the river and over the tips of the dark conifers on the opposite bank.

I go for a walk along the footpath and cycleway that runs along the estuary, utilising the track bed of the former Great Western Railway line, which closed in 1964. There is a bucketful of birdsong from all around, including a cuckoo from somewhere in the distance. Even in the dull light, the colours are beautiful and so autumnal. A lone signal serves as a solitary reminder of what the trail had originally been. I love reminders of the past.

I pass the pub, which I had Googled last night. It's very attractive, dating from 1650. There's a young woman sitting at a table outside, under the veranda, staring into space – not at the view – just at nothing. She's wearing a huge Parka with the hood up, smoking a cigarette. I want to say hello – simply because it's rude not to, but she either doesn't even see me or studiously ignores me.

Back in Eagle One, I start the engine and follow a winding, tree-lined road, which leads to Fairbourne. The morning remains grey, but Fairbourne is greyer. In the dull light, it looks shabby and forlorn. Last year, I saw it as I passed through on the train. My immediate impression was that it was an awful and depressing place. I later reasoned that the train passed through the backs of the various villages and towns, so I was only getting to see the rear of places, the back yards and the bins. But now, as I curb-crawl towards the sea road, the front is indistinguishable from the back. It feels quite desolate and there is a feeling of a timebomb, of something impending... which is uncanny, because Fairbourne is the village that time forgot. Certainly, the village that the local council forgot.

In its insular, island-like location, Fairbourne – along with many places along this and every coast – is taking a battering from the sea. Unlike many places though, the local council have given up on Fairbourne and decided that the sea has won. Newspaper headlines proclaim the village was "lost to the sea" as the "council are planning a *managed retreat*." One report stated the retreat will take *forty years* to complete, so no one needs to dash for their flippers and snorkel. The locals are up in arms, obviously, and there is organised resistance, but considering the geography of its location, the inevitable does seem... inevitable. Fairbourne *feels* like a ghost town and I wonder if the knowledge of its fate instils that.

Fairbourne was another English-made seaside resort, hence its very English name. In the 1880s, Arthur MacDougal of the flour company, bought a plot of land and built a railway station, calling it Fairbourne, despite local opposition to the Englishness of the name. He built a golf course and some houses and Fairbourne was fair born. Despite the late Victorian date for its inception, the majority of Fairbourne looks very much like a modern housing estate.

The village is almost an island, with the sea in front and estuary marshes at the rear. A narrowing spit of land continues out into the Mawddach estuary, towards Barmouth across the water. Fairbourne is perhaps best known for its miniature railway, which runs to the tip of this spit, where it terminates at a handsome station.

Parked near the end of the spit, I have a quick breakfast. I always have fruit first thing in the morning, but I had turned the fridge up the previous day, because it hadn't felt cold enough; as a result, something has gone terribly wrong. A bag of lettuce has turned into what looks like a bag full of the shards of a broken wine bottle. I suck a few frozen grapes, then get an ice cream headache from an apple before abandoning and stepping out into the cold, which is considerably warmer than my breakfast.

It's windy and promising rain. I march through the sandhills and explore the dead end of the peninsula, with views back up the Mawddach estuary to the mountains inland. I then trudge along the pebble ridge crowning the top of the wide, sandy beach. There are "dragon's teeth" along the fringe of the sandhills, running parallel with the sea wall. They are large pyramidical blocks of concrete left over from the war, designed to prevent invasion by tank, as Fairbourne was considered to be a vulnerable target. It still is, but now the sea itself is the enemy.

Two teenage girls are sitting on the concrete sea wall smoking – probably illegally. I can understand how the kids might hate growing up in an isolated community like this. The frequent complaints for such places are that there are no facilities for the youth. Perhaps sitting on the sea wall smoking is as good as it gets.

I'm struck by how cut off and isolated the village feels, surrounded by sea, marsh and mountain, cradled here, well below sea level and very vulnerable. It feels very remote. Many of the houses are bungalows. It looks a bit like a shanty town and it definitely feels condemned.

I come across the first building which isn't a dwelling: an amusement arcade, closed. I do love places out of season; I like the atmosphere. In high season, on a rare good day, this place would probably be crawling. The only problems with visiting out of season are the bad weather and any facilities are closed. There's a bar and grill nearby, but that's also closed. Then the other end of the Fairbourne railway, also closed for the season.

Across the road is the mainline station, next to it is a row of shops. There are a couple of convenience stores, a chippy, an Indian restaurant, all open, all bustling with activity. These shops seem to feature on all the promotional material for the village and I suddenly realise why. It isn't because they're in any way photogenic, because they aren't, but they're one of the very few features in the village which show any form of community. This is the living heart of Fairbourne.

The general store sells everything you could possibly need, including logs, coal and gas, hot drinks and snacks. There's a veranda around the shops with picnic tables under it. People sit there chatting, wrapped up against the cold. Everyone knows everyone. Every person that approaches the shop stops to share a few words with those they pass and they all seem happy and friendly.

As usual, I slip down a couple of side roads which lead to residential streets, where the visitors don't usually go. I find a quiet, suburban, dormitory settlement, a mixture of bungalows and Victorian four and five storey houses. It's very quiet. I don't see anyone at all.

I had read that house prices had plummeted since the news had broken about the watery fate of the village. I actually wondered if I could get a long term rent here very cheaply. I wouldn't mind staying here a finite amount of time. It has something. I think it probably says a lot about me, I'm exploring Britain out of season and am drawn to places that are a bit desolate and have a time limit on them.

Could I live in Fairbourne? As long as it stays on this side of the shoreline, yes, I probably could.

* * * * * * * * * *

As I leave Fairbourne, I encounter an old man driving a huge 4x4 really badly, hunched over the wheel, eyes wide behind his huge glasses. I had also passed him on my way in, when he was driving in a similar state. The weird thing is – and the reason that I recalled him – there is a long orange light on top of the car, like an emergency vehicle would have. The light is possibly to warn other drivers that he's approaching. He shouldn't be behind the wheel of a vehicle, especially not such a large and potentially hazardous vehicle: he's dangerous and a liability. It has nothing to do with his age, but his inability to drive safely.

Less than a minute later, a gormless old bat in a white van starts to pull out in front of me without looking. She stops just in time to avoid a collision. In my rear-view mirror, I can see she's a ruddy-faced farmer's wife-type with a mess of ginger hair. I think she's really shocked because she remains still, gripping the steering wheel as though frozen and she doesn't drive off.

I join the A-road which skirts the headland, with a steep drop down to the sea below. Alarmingly, the low stone wall - that seems to be the only form of barrier between the carriageway and certain death - has been hastily repaired and cobbled together in many places, probably due to Ruddy-Faced Farmer's Wife and Orange Light Man. There are some very tight bends as the road leads away from the coast into green but treeless hills. I can't see either of those deviant drivers coping too well with the bends.

I approach Tywyn, which is very grey; the sky *and* the town. There are lots of concrete sea defences, grey houses, grey-green caravans. On the landward side it's flat, open and bleak. There are no trees at all. In one vast field, the cows are lying down. In a neighbouring field however, a herd of bullocks are clearly wired differently and are all standing. They all seem very sad.

I drive through the town and continue to Aberdyfi, (Aberdovey for the Anglophiles) which literally means the mouth of the river Dyfi. Like Barmouth and pretty much everywhere else I've encountered so far, Aberdyfi was formerly a shipbuilding town, now given over to the tourist trade. The main street is lined with prettily painted gift shops and cosy inns and cafes; it is very much geared towards the tourist, but in a very tasteful and discreet manner. No chips and candyfloss here.

The town has two fronts, one facing the sea, one facing the tidal estuary with views across the Dyfi to the gentler, naked green hills of mid-Wales. I stand watching a flock of oystercatchers on the beach, with their distinctive red legs and curved beaks. A lady with a dog comes up behind me and tells me merrily that there's a seal or an otter about and she's just seen it. I scan the waters for it for a while, but as usual it doesn't show.

The Bells of Aberdovey is a well-known song which tells of the legend of the kingdom of Cantre'r Gwaelod (the Lowland Hundred), which was protected from the sea by dykes and dams. One night, a feast was held and a watchman got drunk and wasn't very watchful. As a result, floodgates were left open and Cantre'r Gwaelod was lost beneath the waves of Cardigan Bay, the bells of which, so the legend goes, can occasionally still be heard ringing. This is certainly true now, as in 2011 a bronze time-and-tide bell was suspended beneath the pier, as an art fixture, which sounds by the action of the waves at high tide, tolling mournfully.

* * * * * * * * * *

Like several other roads in the area, the road leaving Aberdyfi along the Afon Dyfi is undulating and tree-lined, with dangerously tight bends; you can't take your eyes off the road for a minute. Unless you've got a death wish. Unfortunately, many of the oncoming drivers seem to. They are driving too fast for the conditions, making it another very stressful journey. SatNav Sally purposefully tells me to go the wrong way: she tells me to avoid the river crossing and then turn into the river itself. #1 I ignore her – yet again – and cross the river Dyfi by the five graceful arches of the Georgian bridge. This not only takes me across the river, but also across the county boundary, from Gwynedd into Powys.

On the outskirts of Machynlleth, nestling in an old, disused quarry is CAT – the Centre for Alternative Technology, where I spend an inspiring few hours. First, I'm inspired in the vegetarian café – vegetable lasagne and chocolate marble cake (Gorgeous!) then I'm inspired as I wander around the site learning about all aspects of reducing your carbon footprint, as well as saving money on fuel bills. The first pioneers arrived at the derelict former quarry site in 1974 and brought the place back to life. The centre has expanded and developed steadily ever since.

I came here years ago with Nicky. I can't remember too much about it, except in the men's toilets you had to wee into a funnel, which was then collected in a barrel and used for fertilizer. A sign had said something similar about the cubicles as well. Today, while waste may still be used in this way, there is no mention and the toilets are proper urinals and flushing toilets.

There are displays about energy efficiency, transport, green gardening, solar power, wind turbines and much more, but for me the best thing is just wandering around enjoying the greenery and the scenery and the general relaxed vibe. CAT is a template for how the world could be and should be. I return to my diesel-guzzling vehicle feeling full of good intentions. And cake.

* * * * * * * * * * *

I really like the old market town of Machynlleth ("Too many hippies", "Crusties everywhere!", "too many spanish people" (sic), "bitchy people and no nice lads...").

It is famous for its ornate Victorian clock tower, which dominates the centre of town, looking slightly magnificent. Machynlleth – or just plain "Mach" to its friends – clearly has ambitions; it has twice applied for city status, but has so far twice failed.

The town feels lived-in. It is perhaps a little bit grimy in places, but is not unattractive. The streets are wide and lined with bold Victorian buildings and older, some *much* older. One mediaeval hall is known as Owain Glyndŵr's Parliament. Owain was the last native Welshman to hold the title "Prince of Wales". In reality though, this sturdy stone building wasn't built for a century and a half after the man's death.

In 1400, Owain Glyndŵr instigated the Welsh Revolt against the king, Henry IV. After a promising start and many gruesome years of battling, the campaign ultimately foundered and failed. In 1409, Owain fled and spent the rest of his life in hiding. He was twice offered pardons by the new king, the unimaginatively named Henry V, and he twice ignored them. He allegedly died in 1415. Upon his death, he achieved a sort of magical and legendary status, like King Arthur. Owain Glyndŵr is portrayed in Shakespeare's *Henry IV*, as Owen Glendower. He has been hailed as father of Welsh nationalism and he ruled here and then lived in hiding, in and around the would-be city of Machynlleth.

* * * * * * * * * *

<u>If Brendan was with me...</u>

I wouldn't have been allowed in the CAT for a start, not

just because the acronym spells "cat", because Brendan is very tolerant of the feline species. In fact, his brother and sister are both cats. (Hector and Pixie.) It would have been too busy for him. He won't tolerate busyness. Or most things actually.

And for that reason, Brendan would have hated Shell Island. He wouldn't have cared that it was famous for shells, he would have hated every moment. It was too busy, people everywhere, things flapping and swirling, flashing, no privacy, no boundaries. We like our space and we like a bit of seclusion. I suppose that's one of the reasons we're so perfectly suited. But if Shell Island ever do a weekend specifically for grouchy old bastards and their dogs, we'll be there like a shot.

NOTES

#1: You probably think I'm making all the business about SatNav Sally up and I don't blame you. After all, how could a SatNav get it so wrong so much of the time? I mean, constantly telling people to drive into the sea, into rivers and off cliffs... But I swear, not one word is a lie. One day she'll go too far and she'll pay the price. (But that's in the future, another time, another book. I don't want to give too much away; she does indeed feature in *underdogs*, but let's just say she won't be in the sequel.)

ABOVE: The harbour, Shell Island.

ABOVE: Windpump at the Centre for Alternative Technology

CHAPTER 9: ABERMANIA

In which some dangerous prisoners escape – from prison. I visit Welsh Noir country, where I don't get mugged, but I do get shat on from a great height.

My sojourn into Powys is very brief and at some point, unnoticed, I've slipped over the county border into Ceredigion. I'm driving along the other side of the Dyfi estuary back towards the coast. It's another beautiful road, partially through autumnal deciduous woodlands. I love the last few leaves that cling steadfastly to the trees, when most of their comrades have fallen. So many have already been lost, due to the recent storms, so those that remain are even more special and their colours seem that much more important: the copper of the beeches and the yellow of the birches, blowing in the breeze, but not falling. Despite grey skies, there are still moments of rich colour in the landscape.

I reach the end of the peninsula, where the road ends by joining the beach, where there is parking. Two cars are way out on the flat expanse of sand in the middle of the estuary, bumper to bumper, headlight to headlight, wiper to wiper in the pouring rain. It looks like some bizarre Cold War stand-off. People are huddled under umbrellas, seemingly watching this head-to-head. I'd assume they were filming something, but I can't see any cameras or lights. It's very odd. As I drive onto the beach the little congregation all turn and stare at me. The charge for parking here is astronomical and I don't particularly want to stay here long in the pouring rain, so I turn in a circle and drive back towards the exit. The little group all silently watch me, turning their heads in unison as I loop back towards the road. It's all quite unsettling.

The village of Borth, meaning port, is also quite odd. It's a ribbon development along what was once a beach road. It's a mish-mash of styles and colours; there are small ramshackle cottages alongside elegant regency townhouses, tiny terraces, weather-boarded cabins and pebble-dashed semis, some very old, some new, all jammed together. Borth is a bit shabby in places. Some of the colourful guesthouses are somewhat run down, others are immaculate. It's quirky, difficult to define, unusual and I have to say, I really like it. I find its off-beat oddness fascinating.

Yet again, the village has close links with the legend of the prosperous drowned kingdom of Cantre'r Gwaelod, which was consumed by the sea in the 6th Century AD. On the prom, there is a slate sculpture bearing the inscription: "Under the sea and waves lie many a fair city". It's still raining heavily and I'm really starting to feel like the weather is doing its best to put the rest of us underwater as well.

I wander up and down the platform, pretending I'm waiting for a train, but really I'm just soaking up the atmosphere. Borth has a lot of atmosphere. The station no longer has a ticket office, but volunteers have made use of derelict rooms and created the Borth Station Museum, which is full of interesting memorabilia relating to the railway and the town, staffed by friendly and well-informed volunteers. It is definitely worth a visit.

The grasslands that stretch away behind it and the village station itself had featured in the Welsh TV series, *Hinterland*. The *Hinterland* crew took over the station for a week for filming and one of the museum volunteers, George Romary, appeared as an extra, playing a reporter at a press conference. George is friendly and out-going and has a wealth of knowledge about anything and everything local. He tells me the film crew rented a house in the village and many scenes were shot in the area, on the surrounding beaches and using nearby properties and stretches of road. I ask him about the submerged forest which Borth is famous for, and when it might make an appearance. George looks at his watch, then his brow furrows as he mutters about tide times, then he decides it might be partially visible in a short while. I cross to the beach and watch as the stumps of countless trees emerge from the retreating waves. George is bang on! These were trees that lived 5000 or so years ago. It's amazing! (Well, I find it amazing.)

* * * * * * * * * *

I drop down into the lovely town of Aberystwyth – Aber to its friends. ("Scum Bag Townies", "EVERY pub thinks it a sports bar" (sic), "Awful transport", the "Aber trap", "No decent hairdressers", "Smallmindedness....and the F$%*ing Taffia", "Aber apathy".) Aberystwyth is the unofficial capital of Mid Wales. The name literally means "mouth of the river Ystwyth". I park on the seafront and set out in the early evening drizzle to explore.

184

I love Aberystwyth. As a seaside and holiday resort it has everything that is good and traditional, without being in any way tacky. It is an historic and attractive market town and has been a popular tourist destination since the coming of the railway in the Victorian times. It had been known in its heyday as "the Biarritz of Wales." The heart of the town has narrow back streets and colourful regency-style houses and it's a pleasure to wander around exploring, soaking up the atmosphere.

Aber has an incredibly low crime rate. It is a university town, so has a large transitory population of students. Fortunately, it is one of the safest places for students; Wrexham being one of the worst. Generally, mugging is seriously low, with all other crimes low to moderate. (My birthplace, Manchester, as you might expect, has a higher than average crime rate.)

The Victorian pier – the oldest in Wales – was built in 1864. These days it's a bit stubby, some of its length having been washed away by storms. As I walk past, I can hear a constant noise, which at first I assume is the wind whistling through the iron supports beneath the pier. As I get closer, it becomes apparent it's birds. Hundreds of birds. Thousands of birds. I make my way down to the beach and scramble over the pebbles to a deafening avian cacophony. I go right under the pier. I can't see a single bird, they are all concealed in the darkness of the rafters above, but I can hear them all chirruping and chattering away. Then I feel them... as one of them shits on my hand. It's a warning shot. I'm risking a lot being there, so I retreat at speed.

The lights are coming on along the sweep of the promenade and in the town. The headland, Constitution Hill, is in darkness. From the summit, there are views over the whole town and the bay. It's a great walk, but for the less energetic there is a cliff railway to take you to the top, which is the United Kingdom's longest funicular railway.

At the other end of the bay is a lower peninsula, which holds the impressive ruins of Aberystwyth Castle, which is nicely lit on its small headland. A ghostly white figure walks ethereally in front of its crumbling walls, through the beams of one of the spotlights and then disappears. It's possibly a ghost, but more probably just a person in a white coat. It's windy on the castle hill. Three youths are slouching sulkily along one of the paths, trying to look menacing with the hoods of their hoodies up. When I remain walking towards them, they turn round and scuttle off at speed.

I walk the length of the promenade. It's very quiet. There are one or two people walking along, faces screwed up against the rain. The waves roll in along the deserted beach. There are numerous footprints in the sand from earlier in the day. Although tonight's tide is benign, Aber has suffered its fair share of batterings from the sea. One night in January 1938, a storm struck the town, destroying most of the promenade and 200 feet of the pier. It was badly hit again in January 2014, tearing up boulders from the sea walls and causing devastation.

The fine Victorian town houses along the front are very similar to Llandudno; their bright colours and warm lighting make them look very inviting. I ask myself a question I always ask of any place: could I see myself living here? I'm not at all surprised when I answer myself with a firm and unequivocal "Yes!". I could *definitely* see myself living here.

* * * * * * * * * * *

Again, I have nowhere to stay the night. I've tried several car parks and laybys recommended on a wild camping website, but all had hostile signs: STRICTLY NO OVERNIGHT CAMPING. OFFENDERS WILL BE PROSECUTED, and even NO CAMPER VANS ALLOWED TO PARK HERE AFTER 11PM. The general rule is, you can only stay the night where there are no signs telling you not to. It doesn't guarantee you won't be moved on by the police, but it does mean you won't be prosecuted. That's how I understand it anyway. If I end up finishing this account from a prison cell, then I was wrong.

I drive around Aberystwyth, following a sign for "De South", which doesn't sound at all Welsh to me. I give up looking for a car park to stay overnight in and flick through my site book. I find one a couple of miles away at a golf club. The friendly and trusting chap on the phone gives me verbal instructions and tells me to pay in the morning, when the club house is open. I find the site and park in a small car park next to some bins. Nice. It's pitch black and quite isolated, but I feel happy and relieved that I'm not going to be told to move.

I have curry in a tin for tea and go to sleep listening to the rain.

* * * * * * * * * * *

The next morning is like another day, which indeed it is. It's fine and sunny. In daylight, the golf course is lovely. I hadn't seen any of it last night and the area I'd been told to go to, next to the bins, was definitely the worst spot. The nice lady in the club house says the wind and rain had kept her awake in the night and she kept thinking the roof was coming off. "It must have been worse for you in a van." she very thoughtfully adds, but it hadn't really disturbed me.

Back en route, the scenery around Aberystwyth is beautifully autumnal: patchwork fields and pockets of trees. I have side-lights on, but the approaching traffic has full headlights blazing, which is ominous. As I head ever-south, there are fewer trees. The landscape is still nice and green, but it's mainly grassy fields now, wider, open and exposed.

The road is undulating, with some fairly steep climbs. I notice, for the first time ever, that Eagle One is struggling with the gradients. She has never been like this before. She seems to be mis-firing, occasionally sluggish, but only when accelerating on an incline. I'm a bit concerned. I decide it's probably better if I stop and have a cup of tea – that's bound to help – so I pull into a layby. It's high up and I have a brief view down over sloping fields to the gunmetal grey of the sea, before the windows are suddenly blurred with violent, hammering rain.

The lovely weather from the morning has definitely gone now. For good. My cup of tea is nice, but strangely, hasn't really helped the van situation. I press on anyway, accelerating up the hills, but quite slowly.

Llannon is a small village of painted terrace houses, in every shade imaginable. It is synonymous with the so-called "Rebecca Riots". They took place in the mid-1800's and were protests by local farmers in opposition to unfair taxation. The leader of the first protest wore women's clothes and the rumour is that they belonged to a woman called Rebecca, hence their adopted name. The dress supposedly represented the Welsh judicial system and wasn't just an excuse to cross-dress at the weekend.

Once outside the village, we sail along smoothly on the downhill runs and judder slowly on the uphill stretches, until we reach the little town of Aberaeron. The main street is very attractive: again it's all Regency terraces painted different colours, which seems to be the norm in these parts. Apart from the gleefully painted houses everywhere, the colour I'm seeing most of today is grey; I know I can't keep saying "grey sea, grey sky, grey tarmac" – you get the picture. The grey picture. I've decided I'll need to be more specific and descriptive with my greys.

I wander along the beach in the bullet grey rain. There is a concrete-grey sea wall protecting the insidious pebble-dashed grey council houses and a barrier of huge, steel-grey rocks have been dumped in a line along the edge of the beach. Call me cynical, but I wonder whether the bad houses have been built near the shore because if there's encroachment from the sea, the poorer people in the cheaper houses will be the first affected.

The sky is seal grey, but the sea is a one-shot latte brown.

There is a clear divide today between grey sky and brown sea, because the colours are so different. It looks very odd, surreal.

An old man is sitting in a shelter on the sea wall, calmly reading a newspaper while the wind and rain rage around him. His wispy hair is a fine, powder-grey; his fingertips a dark charcoal from the newsprint. He seems very at peace in the elements, probably grateful for this time away from whatever stresses await him at home.

* * * * * * * * * * *

I arrive in the Welsh harbour town of New Quay, or in Welsh *Cei Newydd,* which translates – perhaps not surprisingly – as *New Quay.* It was a fishing village and then a shipbuilding town – like everywhere else on this coast – then it turned its hand to tourism once holidays had been invented.

Walking through New Quay today is like walking through the wild west. Only wetter. Trees and shrubs are thrashing violently, garden gates are banging repeatedly, telephone wires are clacking overhead. There are no birds in sight and very few people about. It's a very clean village, so I'm robbed of the spectacle of, say, a newspaper whipping along the street, tumbleweed-style.

Nearly all the shops are closed. A shell shop is open, though I'm not sure why, it's on a quiet street and there's no one about to enter. And all it sells is seashells. On the seashore.

I walk up steep back streets, trying to get a feel for the place. The village was originally called something else and took its name, predictably, from the *new quay* that was built here. The town increased in size as a workforce of three hundred men were brought in to work in the shipbuilding industry. The land above the harbour is lined with pastel-painted terrace houses, built to provide homes for the men and their families.

New Quay has a legitimate link with the work of Dylan Thomas, who lived in the area in the mid-Fifties. It is often claimed the town was the inspiration for the village of Llareggub in *Under Milk Wood.* The village name it isn't a proper Welsh word; it means bugger all.*

* Literally. Read it backwards.

On leaving New Quay, the road is awash with sandy soil-coloured water, which is bubbling up from all the grids, which obviously can't cope with the deluge. The sky ahead is the colour of graphite. Specifically, the shade of a well-worn HB7 pencil. It really isn't the best weather to experience these places.

I pass some roadworks. Two poor young work-youths are standing in the piss-pouring rain turning the STOP/GO lollipops. I feel for them as I drive past in my warm, cosy van. They look really miserable.

I drive around Aberporth looking for a place to stay the night. Apart from a sandy beach, it's home to *RAF Aberporth*. It has an air and sea danger area, still in operation, which was used for testing air and sea-launched missiles. The camp closed in 1984 and the site became a centre for the testing of unmanned aircraft, for both military and civilian use. Drones regularly criss-cross the skies around Aberporth on manoeuvres. The

"Watchkeeper" unmanned aerial vehicle is known locally as "the Flying Lawnmower" due to the noise of its engine. I don't see or hear any… but then, I can barely see or hear anything, due to the constant hammering rain.

The narrow lanes around Aberporth are flooded right across at several points. A brook has burst its bank and is flowing directly onto the road. The rain is unending and is starting to feel like a biblical deluge. Everything is starting to feel a bit cataclysmic and borderline "end of days".

I find a campsite, but it's all locked up. No one answers the office door bell or the phone, so I reluctantly drive on towards Cardigan. The on-coming cars have had their headlights on full beam all day. By 2.30 it looks like dusk. It's raining so hard and the clouds are low. It's a terrible, wet, windy day. And I love it!

I get a text from Nicky: a warning. Why is it that whenever I go away a murderer or seriously dangerous person escapes from prison? This has happened several times before and I'm starting to feel paranoid. People who know me must think I go away doing jail breaks. I don't. (Unless the money's right, in which case: call me!)

In 1953, HMP Spring Hill, not in the area, became the first open prison for men in Britain. Perhaps a bit too open. Over the past week, apparently, three inmates have escaped on three different days. One is a murderer and one threatened a partially blind man with secateurs at his throat. Nicky is panicking in case they hop into my van at night. I have to promise I will take extra care in choosing sites from now on.

* * * * * * * * * * *

The wild-camping website recommended a car park in the centre of Cardigan, where you could pay to stay overnight. It sounds ideal and has good reviews. I have a quick drive round the rain-wet town and find the car park, right next to the River Teifi, which has signs warning of flooding. The river does look very swollen. I choose a parking bay as far from the water as possible. The car park isn't overlooked by any premises, which is good from a "not pissing the locals off" point of view, but less good from a "being murdered by escaped convicts" standpoint. I go to buy my overnight parking ticket from the pay and display machine. I decide, for some reason, to read the bylaws in small print on the sign. It looks as though it's all legit and above board, until the very last line, when it states IT IS ILLEGAL TO STAY OVERNIGHT IN VEHICLES. OFFENDERS WILL BE PROSECUTED. I'm really frustrated, because most of the information I'm relying on from the website is either out of date or just plain wrong. I drive off in a right mood.

I check my campsite book, make a few calls and eventually find a site a couple of miles out of the town, run by a lovely middle-aged couple. She's English with a plummy accent, he's a gruff Welshman with a big beard and an accent so thick it could be used to make a very effective draught excluder. His English is unfathomable; it sounds more foreign than his Welsh, but he keeps smiling, so I assume he's being friendly. They have a campsite and a series of self-catering cottages, formerly barns and outbuildings, set in very attractive grounds. The campsite proper is closed for the season, so the lady tells me to park in a courtyard for shelter from the wind and rather than opening the toilet block I should use the bathroom of a vacant self-catering cottage. She shows me around it. "Use the telly, use the kitchen... Wash up in here... Use the microwave... The heating's on anyway, so you might as well make use of it. The bathroom has a corner bath and shower. All I ask is that you keep it tidy."

She charges me ten pounds. I say it isn't enough for all this luxury. She eventually takes fifteen, but returns a few minutes later bearing a refund, saying her husband told her a tenner was more than enough. "Stay longer, if you like. It's a good location for exploring the coast. The cottage isn't booked until the weekend."

I'm not too sure when the weekend is, but it's evidently several days away. Nicky will be very pleased I'm staying somewhere so safe and secure. I have a nice hot shower and even wash my pots in a proper sink – with *hot* water; it's like a holiday for them. Outside, the wind is ferocious and the rain is pelting down, but I'm sheltered and safe... Unless the escaped killers come to South Wales in search of holiday cottage accommodation.

* * * * * * * * * * *

7am. The alarm goes off. It isn't raining. 7.05am. It starts to rain.

It's so bitterly cold. I lie in bed looking at the kettle, willing it to boil. But that doesn't work. Someone's going to have to get up and switch it on – and it's probably going to be me.

I sit up in bed to drink my tea, hoodie on, hood up, a

blanket around my shoulders. It was so mild yesterday, I can't believe the sudden drop in temperature. It's freezing. I have a feeling I'm doing too much driving and not seeing enough of this beautiful part of the country. As a result, I book onto the site until Saturday... though I'm still not sure when that is... Because of the peninsular nature of the coastline here, I can explore a good distance without moving too far away from this site

I drive back to Cardigan, or Aberteifi as it's called in Welsh, which we should all know by now, means the "mouth of the river Teifi". The river looks dangerously high as I park up in that same car park that had so pissed me off yesterday. I wrap up and go for a walk around the old town, where there is a biting wind blasting along the narrow streets. People are walking with their hoods up, heads down, hands in pockets; the elderly people in particular are hunched up, trying to keep their feet on the pavement. I become aware that people seem to be staring at me in a strange way. Am I being paranoid? Yes, I am generally paranoid by nature; it's one of my most endearing qualities. But they really are staring in a disturbing manner, not in the usual way that people stare. I decide it's probably because I've got my hoodie up; I do look a bit sinister and they might be thinking I'm one of the escaped convicts.

A man is dawdling along in front of me, looking in the shop windows. His head is shaved at the sides but with a shock of spikey hair on top, which makes him look like a pineapple. This would be fine, except his head is the same shape and size as a large pineapple, so it's very odd. I become aware that we're both stopping at the same shop windows and keep overtaking each other. I'm sure

I wouldn't even have been aware of him, except for his distinctive pineapple head.

I lose sight of Pineapple Head, then bump into him again. Continually. It's starting to get embarrassing. I try to avoid him by turning off the high street, only to bump into him coming towards me. It's getting really awkward, so I duck into a café for a breakfast. It's relatively quiet, but a woolly-haired Welshman comes and sits at the nearest table, facing me. I pick up from stilted snatches of conversations he has with the waitress, that he usually meets his friend here, but today his friend is somewhere else, so he occupies himself by staring directly at me the whole time he eats his breakfast. Then bloody Pineapple Head appears at the till to pay his bill. He's been in here the whole time. I give him plenty of time to get away before I venture outside. I still fully expect to see him, but I don't.

I wander through the tight old streets of Cardigan. It's a pleasant and genuine old town, compact and unpretentious. I'm glad when I get back to the car park to find it hasn't flooded and the tide is obviously going out. Today appears to be Cardigan's day when all the pensioners who don't drive/won't drive/couldn't drive/ shouldn't drive come out in their little cars to do their shopping. The streets are filled with them, gripping the steering wheels, peering over the dashboard, glowering in fury or in a state of panic with wide eyes, not indicating, trying to park for an hour and a half and holding up the whole of the traffic in south Wales. If it wasn't so dangerous it would be comical. But it isn't comical, it's dangerous, and I don't laugh.

I cross over the Teifi and drive through various small villages and hamlets, the road winding and climbing, with views over the countryside and over the dark, dramatic, cliffs to the sea. There are blue skies! (Apart from the rainclouds.) Then I'm coasting downhill towards Newport. I don't have my foot on the accelerator for most of the way. I feel very laid back and at peace, enjoying the scenery and the sense of freedom.

I park on a wide bridge crossing over the tidal estuary near Newport. The tide is out and on the mud flats there are wading birds, including the instantly recognisable oystercatchers with their black and white plumage, but also a solitary curlew with its distinctive, long curved beak. It's a nasty curlew, far bigger than the Oystercatchers, and he keeps needlessly strutting up to them and pecking at them, so they flutter a few feet away.

Newport – I've no idea where the port in question is, because I don't find one – is a quiet, attractive village with a few nice shops, a few nice pubs and of course a few hairdressers. Rather oddly, there's a wholefood deli, where I buy a little marzipan stollen for £2. I'm not sure exactly what a stollen is, but it's a cake, so what can go wrong?

According to the OS map, there's an ancient site in the village, which I eventually find in a small fenced field amongst a quiet cul-de-sac of houses. It's a chambered cairn, an impressive structure made up of four massive upright stones with a huge capstone, which only resting on two of the uprights; it looks quite precarious, but it has survived several thousand years so far, so I don't think I need to worry.

As I approach, I see a man with a long grey beard in an old-fashioned raincoat with the hood up, which is a bit like a cloak, so he looks like a wizard. Despite the grey beard he isn't some gnarled ancient; he looks like he's probably in his thirties. He's touching the stones and his head is bowed in silent prayer or meditation. I don't think he's aware of me, as he's so lost in the moment. I wait at the gate to give him some time and some space; when eventually he looks up and sees me he's suddenly very embarrassed. I say hello, but he just smiles a very tight-lipped smile of resentment. The earth doesn't open up and swallow him, despite his wishes.

I walk round the cairn, marvelling at the size and trying to imagine how the Neolithic people had moved these stones here and got them into place. There is a huge overhanging holly bush, so the capstone and the ground around is spattered with deep red berries, like droplets of blood, which seems very symbolic, as this was once a tomb.

Merlin is still standing in the corner, clearly waiting for me to move on, so he can resume his ceremony. I look at him to say goodbye, but he's pretending to be on his mobile phone. This looks ludicrous and incongruous and not at all Druidic or New Age! I leave him to it.

I arrive back at Eagle One for a tea and some stollen. I start off thinking the stollen is a bit odd, not sure what to make of it, but after my eighth piece I'm hooked. I have icing sugar all over my muzzle and to anyone glancing in I must look like a drooling, cocaine-crazed maniac. I eat half the loaf. It's only small, an ant could carry it off without calling for his friends to help. Although he probably would call them anyway, because ants are team players.

* * * * * * * * * *

Ynys Dinas/Dinas Island comes into view along the main road, a mass of rock topped with grass. It's actually an island, hence its name, but I'm not aware of the join, which is apparently essentially marshland rather than a body of proper common-or-garden water. I decide to walk along the footpath around the perimeter of the island, which is part of the Pembrokeshire Coastal Path.

There are a few houses and a church and not a lot else. I set off along a footpath and pass a friendly, elderly Welsh chap working in his garden. He calls across: "It's gone cold! My finger's frozen!"

I stop and look at him, confused. "Sorry?" He sounds distressed and I'm not sure whether he's injured himself... or possibly escaped from somewhere.

"My finger!" He holds up a finger. (That's "*a* finger", not "*the* finger".) "I broke it and it's frozen. It doesn't half feel the cold now. I just can't get it warm!" He'd lived here, in this remote and secluded spot for 52 years, he tells me. He seems very proud of the fact that in all that time he's only been snowed in on two occasions, so it's generally quite mild. I tell him to keep his finger warm, bid him farewell and continue along the path, leading steeply uphill between trees. The trees end and the landscape opens out onto a grassy headland with the sea far below and views back to all the places I've visited earlier. Impressive cliffs stretch away into the distance, with various prominent headlands competing for amazingness. Most of them are neck and neck.

The sun is starting to set, which is a bit worrying. I know it goes down every day, so I shouldn't be surprised, but it's a whole lot earlier than I expected. *And* much earlier than is convenient. The sunset isn't an exact time; it depends where you are and where and what your horizon is. Here, the horizon is the edge of the sea, so I have maximum available sunage. Even so, the light seems to be fading much too fast and I don't want to stumble over the cliff edge in the dark. Or in the light, for that matter. I quicken my pace: moving up a gear from "brisk stride" to "frantic trot".

The path splits and a little map illustrates the two routes available. The green route is the safe path, along the edge of the fields; the red route is the dangerous, narrow, steep, close-to-the-cliff-edge "Path of Death". As it's getting dark and is cold and windy there's only really one choice. Yes, I choose the red "Path of Death".

So, my friends, if this is the last page in the book, I obviously didn't make it. But thanks for joining me on this journey, it's been great!

We hope you have enjoyed this book.

(Possibly)
THE END.

* * * * * * * * * *

Well, as there's another page it obviously means I survived... or this travelogue is being completed by a ghost writer. Spooky.

I stand at the tip of Ynys Dinas, looking down on what I assume is Needle Rock. A pinnacle. A rock stack with the sea seething and crashing around it. It makes a good roosting place for sea birds. There are panoramic views over Cardigan Bay and out to the horizon, where the sun is sinking and fading fast.

I'm trying my best to hurry, but unfortunately, thirty-six hours of rain has turned the narrow pathway into coffee-coloured Angel Delight. It isn't so much dangerous, as really hard work and time consuming as I slide all over the place. My feet are slipping *and* sticking... which isn't even possible... It's like walking through treacle... Walking very, very slowly through very slippery treacle. (Which would be best served in a shortcrust pastry flan case.)

The views along the cliffs are spectacular and remind me of Cornwall. I'm overwhelmed by that feeling of awe and inspiration, the acknowledgement that it really is a beautiful country we live in.

I arrive at the highest part of Dinas Island, the white Trig Point at 466 feet. I step cautiously to the very end of the peninsula and look down warily at the sea pummelling the rocks below. I have only moved a matter of yards from the Trig Point, but when I turn around there is a middle-aged couple standing there.

"Oh... Where did you two appear from?" I ask, startled.

"The path. Down there." the woman says, a little clipped, pointing in the opposite direction to the way I'd come. "Where did *you* come from?"

The man just smiles: not so much in a friendly way, but in a "yes, my wife has a very brusque tone" manner.

"That way." I point towards the rocks of Dinas Head. "Did it take you long to get here? I just want to make sure I get back before dark."

"Half an hour or so." the man says, still smiling.

"Where are you from?" the woman asks suddenly, in the tone of a school teacher or prison warder.

"Near Manchester."

She sighs. "Where*abouts*?"

"South Manchester."

She sounds increasingly cross. "Where *specifically*?"

"Oh…"

"Go on…" the man cajoles, "Just answer her."

"Stockport."

"I thought so!" she says triumphantly. "That's where I'm from!"

From that moment on she's lovely. We've bonded. We talk for a few minutes about places we know and how things have changed; how some places have changed and that's a bad thing, and how some places *hadn't* changed and that's *also* a bad thing, because they really ought to have.

He's from Wiltshire; they had met when he had been working in Stockport. They had taken early retirement and moved to Pembrokeshire. He harbours "this crazy idea" that he wants to walk the whole of the Pembrokeshire Coastal Path. "Not all in one go, obviously! Just a bit at a time."

I tell them about my trip around the coast. They get very excited, telling me about places to visit and places to eat around Pembrokeshire.

"You should definitely come to Dale, where we live. It's lovely."

I tell them I'll be going through it on my way to the Saint Ann's Head peninsula. This excites them to melting point.

"You must stop in Dale! There's so much to see! D'you know what... you should stay overnight!"

"Oh..." I steel myself, ready to politely refuse their kind offer of hospitality. "That's very..."

"In the car park. The public car park. The one near the beach. It's free overnight. Never any problem."

"Oh..." I wasn't expecting that. "Right..." I'm both relieved and offended. "Well, I might do." (I won't.)

It's gone very cold and very blustery and is rapidly getting darker. I thank them for the information and for their kind offer of accommodation – in a public car park – then we go our separate ways.

* * * * * * * * * * *

I spend another relaxing night basking in the heat and enjoying the luxurious facilities of my holiday cottage, returning to Eagle One only to sleep. I wake up the next morning freezing cold. The day picks up, the sun comes out and there is a beautiful blue sky.

I drive southwest again, towards the coast, calling into a local garage for fuel. It's a few pence dearer than the chains, but that's OK – I'd rather be independent. I buy some independent bread as well, from a local bakery. It tastes considerably less capitalist than normal bread.

I veer off the main road, following signs for another burial chamber. They direct me along lanes, winding and getting narrower, with hedges getting higher; each turning takes me down a narrower lane. Eventually I arrive at a parking bay. There are views all around over farmland and hills soaked in sunshine. Another car arrives in the layby. I just hope it isn't Merlin from yesterday. As I'm struggling into my wellies, there's a loud noise, like a stone crash. I can only imagine it's Merlin and he's put too much weight on the stones whilst hugging them and they've crashed down around him like oversized dominoes. They've survived for millennia, but less than a minute of Merlin. But it *isn't* Merlin. It's a woman with two noisy children. I don't know what the noise was, but all the stones seem to be in place.

The monument is very impressive, another series of uprights with a huge capstone. It is set in a most inspiring location, with views over the rolling lowland landscape to a big stone-topped mountain in the background. This is somewhere in the Prescelli hills, which I've read about many times, where the "bluestones" from Stonehenge came from. The original theory was that the eighty or so monoliths were quarried in this area and were carried by raft along the coast and into the Bristol Channel, where they were transported to Salisbury Plain and erected around 2900 to 2300 BC. Current thinking, though, is that the stones were the unwitting passengers of a roving glacier, left behind on Salisbury Plain when the glacier eventually melted. Whichever the case, I find it fascinating.

* * * * * * * * * *

Driving back to the main road, I take a wrong turning and end up on a single-track lane with high banks on either side, so high it's like going through a tunnel cut into the earth. If any vehicle approaches there's no way for them to pass and no way to turn round. I'm committed now to continuing straight ahead. Fortunately, no traffic does approach and the lane widens slightly as it nears the main road. A telecom engineer is working on a telegraph pole and his van is blocking most of the road. I manage to edge cautiously past, but just touch his mirror with mine, but no harm is done. He looks at me; his eyes say: "Oi, you've clipped me fucking mirror!" *My* eyes say: "Well, shift your van then!" But that remains as a subtext. He smiles and pushes his mirror in and I give him a thumbs-up and drive slowly away.

The descent into Fishguard is tight and steep. At the bottom it becomes a very narrow road, so narrow in fact that it virtually passes through the houses, which open directly onto the street. There is even a small pub, the door of which opens onto this A-road. I'm surprised there aren't many incidents here when drunken people stagger out at night directly into a moving vehicle. Perhaps there are.

Fishguard fell foul to many Viking raids in its history and its English name is Norse. That doesn't make much sense, but in Welsh the town is known as Abergwaun, which, as you well know, means the mouth of the River Gwaun. The town is divided into two parts, the older part, Lower Fishguard and the main town is called just Fishguard, not Upper or Higher Fishguard.

I wander through Fishguard-the-Upper, which is nicer than I expected. I've been before with Nicky, maybe a quarter of a century ago. We didn't like it very much then, but I'm not sure why. It's mainly made up of Georgian and Victorian buildings in the town centre and a shed-load of them are listed. There are some very lovely cottages and houses and a few nice pubs as well. Although it's only 11.30, most of the pubs seem to be open.

I follow a footpath signed as a marine walk, which takes me steeply downhill through woodland and eventually leads to the harbour in Lower Fishguard. Across the still water, there are a row of coloured cottages. It all looks very tranquil... except that from my vantage point it looks remarkably like the setting for *The Wicker Man*.

I walk along the arm of the quay. Across the bay I can see the next port of Goodwick, where a huge Stenna Line ship is unloading. It looks incongruous and out of place, way too large to be in this little corner of south Wales. There is a thunder-like rattle as lorries trundle off the ship.

Workmen have got a cherry picker on the quay at Fishguard and are putting strings of coloured lights up for Christmas, which – on a sunny day like today – looks ridiculous. Up on the headland above this peaceful harbour, are the ruins of Fishguard Fort, which was built in 1779 after a pirate raid. The resolute people of Fishguard refused to pay a ransom of £1,000, so the pirates bombarded the town.

Despite the fort overlooking the bay, Fishguard was the site of the last "successful" invasion of Britain. In 1797, 1,400 French soldiers landed nearby. They were allegedly "startled" when they saw local women in traditional Welsh dress and, bizarrely, they surrendered two days later. A peace treaty was signed in the Royal Oak pub in the market square; we know this because in large letters above the door it proudly proclaims: LAST INVASION OF BRITAIN PEACE TREATY WAS SIGNED HERE IN 1797.

Across the road is the modest Georgian town hall, formerly a market hall. On display inside is the Fishguard Tapestry, which aims to emulate the Bayeux Tapestry. It was unveiled in 1997 to mark the 200th anniversary of the Last Invasion.

* * * * * * * * * *

On leaving Fishguard, I have another big row with Satnav Sally. She tells me it will take three hours to get to my next destination, Strumble Head, which is a few miles along the coast. In the end, I fling her into the dark of the glove compartment, which has never been used to store gloves in.

I can see the Strumble Head lighthouse from miles away, across rough fields with scrubby hedges, dotted with hardy sheep. I follow the lanes towards it: I rumble to Strumble. I park in the clifftop car park. It's a landscape of gorse, heather and sheep-cropped grass, with black cliffs dropping down to the sea. The lighthouse dominates the area. It was built in 1908, one of the last to be built in Britain. It stands on an island off the headland and is linked to the mainland via a bridge, but there is no access for the public. Strumble Head's light signature is four flashes followed by eight seconds of darkness, so the whole cycle is repeated four times a minute. Each lighthouse has its own unique signature, so mariners can deduce their location.

Little white ponies appear around Eagle One, nibbling on the grass. They seem to be wild, but are far from livid. They're obviously very used to being around people, grazing in a very relaxed manner.

I head down to a low white building on the cliff edge. It looks somewhat militaristic and turns out to be a former coast guard look out which has been converted into a sealife observation post. It was opened in 1988 by Springwatch TV naturalist, Bill Oddie. I learn from the display boards that I've already seen some lesser black-backed gulls and that Strumble Head is one of the best places in Britain to view cetaceans like whales, dolphins and porpoise. The gannet is Britain's largest sea bird, which stands to reason. Basking sharks and grey seals are also regularly spotted from here.

I do seal watch. Nothing. I do seal and dolphin watch.

Nothing. I do seal, dolphin and porpoise watch. Nothing. I'm starting to think this sea is completely empty, when suddenly... No... it's empty.

I stay until the sun's gone down and the after-work joggers and dog walkers are arriving.

* * * * * * * * * * *

If Brendan was with me...

He would probably have caught a taxi home. It was too wet and too windy for him. Besides, he has a very strict "no escaped convicts" policy. With murderers on the loose I may have felt some comfort having my dog with me. But what am I saying? In the event of any form of attack, he would have used me as a human shield.

Brendan would have loved the holiday cottage and the warmth and comfort, but getting him to return to the van at night to sleep might have caused some serious problems.

ABOVE: The beach, Borth.

ABOVE: Burial chamber, Newport.

ABOVE: Trig Post, Ynys Dinas.

CHAPTER 10: THE SMALLEST CITY

In which I get around. I meet heroes and villains, and go on a roadtrip with the Beach Boys. I also visit the smallest city... and find it closed.

So, it's a Saturday today. Apparently. Days tend to go out of the window when you're living life free on the open road, restricted only by hunger pangs and the threat of killers on the loose.

I feel uncomfortable leaving the site without saying goodbye and thanking my hosts for their kindness, their local advice and their hot water, but I also don't want to disturb them. Although I'd assume country folk would usually be up early, walking around in green wellies, all the curtains of their house are closed and there is a soporific stillness about it. Besides, I've left them a nice message in the visitors' book in the cottage, but as I drive past their house I think I see the woman walking along the driveway. I honk the horn and wave frantically, but when she turns round, startled, I see that it isn't her at all; a strange woman stares back and then starts walking very quickly away - a pace that's bordering on running. But she doesn't *actually* break into a full run and she doesn't scream, so I feel a bit proud.

I have enjoyed my three nights at the cottage; I have enjoyed having a base to go back to. I have enjoyed not having to make countless phone calls after dark trying to find a site. I have enjoyed not having to check out countless dodgy laybys and car parks. Most of all, I have enjoyed having access to a hot shower and a heated towel rail! But at the same time, it has felt a bit like cheating. It has all felt a little bit too safe. Now I'm happy to be travelling properly to pastures new. Driving along the open road and not knowing exactly where I will end up next has its own kind of thrill and the day is filled with good vibrations. I could find myself literally *anywhere* in this whole world – as long as it's coastal, anti-clockwise and in the region of Saint David's.

There's currently some sunshine, but there are dark clouds in the sky. I'm on a wide-open road and the landscape feels wide-open. It feels good. This feels like a roadtrip. Today, I'm on a surfin' safari with the Beach Boys – by which I mean singin' about surfin', not actually doin' it. Just like 80% of the Beach Boys.

Eagle One is performing better today on the gradients. I did a bit of internet research and have decided it might be an oil filter problem, hence losing power on acceleration. Anyway, no issues today so far. Isn't it disappointing when everything goes right?

* * * * * * * * * * * *

I arrive mid-morning at Porthgain: I'm surprised it isn't called Aber-something (insert unpronounceable name of local river), then I realise it doesn't seem to have a river.

It's *afon*-free. It does, however, have a harbour, hence its actual name: Porthgain, meaning beautiful port. This is an odd name for a rather industrial little harbour, though the industry is historic, so that's acceptable. In 1987, it was designated as a conservation area. Dyslexics regularly come here to chat.

The harbour is small, high-walled and rather severe, built into a rocky cove. The sea is swelling and surging with awesome might. It's very windy and bitterly cold. The export used to export slate from local quarries. When the slate industry declined, industrious Porthgain turned its hand to brickmaking.

A set of steps lead up to the cliffs, where there are views across countless inlets and along the coast. I can see Strumble Head in the distance, flashing its distinctive signature. The sea is wild, thrashing against the rocks and exploding in the inlets. The flat plain behind the cliffs is littered with remains connected with the quarrying. I have a brief look around them, but it's almost too windy to stand up, so I return to the village. Porthgain is a small settlement of sturdy houses, brick and painted plaster. There's also a pub, *The Sloop*, named after a type of boat. It puts me in mind of the Beach Boys, because of their single, *Sloop John B*. A sign outside says NO PUB CRAWLERS THANK YOU.

The inn was formerly called the *Step In*, because boats were able to dock beside the pub and the crews could literally "step in". I step in and order a black coffee. The pub is suitably old fashioned and full of character. The walls are filled with photographs of the village and the port in the "glory days". My coffee arrives, brought by a pleasant Eastern European chap. I was expecting a standard cup, but instead I'm handed a gigantic mug of strong black coffee. A second one would have killed me, but one merely causes superficial damage and light injury.

The coffee, the clifftop scenery and the views are spectacular, but the harbour and the industrial architecture are what really make Porthgain something a bit different.

* * * * * * * * * * *

It has become very sunny, but with a strong, cold breeze. Driving along with the window up, it's like a Caribbean summer; with the window down, it's like an Arctic winter. I'm heading along banked lanes towards Saint David's Head at the tip of the peninsula. There are occasional outcrops of gorse, but very few trees and only the occasional house. In the distance, is a prominent hill with a noticeable, bare-backed, rocky summit. Though it's only 181 metres high, because it's isolated it completely dominates the whole area. This is Carn Llidi, which translates as *Cairn of the Gates* or *Cairn of Wrath*, either of which sounds powerful and mystical. I can imagine that Stone Age peoples feared and worshipped it. It looks very dramatic, very fearful and very worshipful. I would fear and worship it myself but I'm pushed for time.

The road terminates at the car park for the aptly named Whitesands Bay, which is full of camper vans and people in wet suits. (These are surfers, not rubber fetishists. Presumably.) The beach is beautiful, as its name suggests. The sea is full of surfing dudes who have come to catch a wave. The bay has that California feelin': rolling waves and golden sand sheltering beneath the rocky headland of Saint David's Head. All it needs is the warmth of the sun, unfortunately there is a biting wind and just watching the surfers makes me shiver. There are stunning views out to sea, the kind of views that make you feel very small compared to the vastness of the ocean.

I set off on foot along the path to the headland. Within minutes the seaside clamour of the beach, the laughter, the joyful shouting and the ice cream, is left behind and I'm engulfed in a lonely landscape of sheep-cropped grass, heather and gorse. I look back along the coast and watch the sea crashing into the base of the cliffs, sending white spray up a dozen or more feet. I realise I'm thinking about my former work and am quite stressed and agitated. Although I want this trip to be about exorcising the past and trying to find a path for the future, this isn't the right time. Perhaps there *isn't* a right time. Perhaps there never will be. But right now, I'm in a beautiful place, the surf's up and I want to enjoy the moment, the views, the clean air. I decide to try and stop this train of thought, so I start to smile; it's a forced smile, but it's a smile nevertheless. That helps a bit, but it isn't enough. I start whistling a jaunty, somewhat karaoke version of *California Girls* - because it's topical - and I get caught by two couples who appear from nowhere and stare at me as though I'm one of the missing murderers, which, I say again, I'm not.

The smiling and whistling does the trick. Feeling a lot happier, but a bit embarrassed, I reach the very tip of St David's Head, which is well-worth the walk. There are views in every direction, back along the coast I had previously visited, ahead along the coast I have yet to visit and across the surging waves to Ramsey Island, a hulking great island which is now an RSPB bird sanctuary.

It struck me yesterday, it's November, so it's also "Movember", when men are encouraged to grow a weird moustache and raise money for men's health charities. I haven't seen a single moustache so far – until now. Someone passes me on the path who has a moustache. Fortunately, it's a man. It's a very odd moustache, which makes me think it's probably almost definitely a Movember moustache. I want to ask the chap about it and congratulate him, but don't want to offend him in case it's *not* a Movember moustache and this odd hirsuteage is just how he chooses to have his moustache. I looked into Movember once, with a view to getting all the males at work to do it *en masse*. The thing is, you have to choose from a small range of moustaches – and they're all rather silly, ostentatious and embarrassing, so you end up making a fool of yourself. That's sort of the point really. It's supposed to be fun and provide a talking point. Strangers might come up to you and ask if you're doing it for Movember or if there's something wrong with you. For me it all presented too much of an ordeal. The final nail in the coffin of Movember, as far as work was concerned, was that you have to start off with a completely shaved face. I have a goatee – to be without it would be like going into work naked. (Naked Work Fridays didn't catch on either.)

Anyway, looking down on Whitesands Bay, the surfer guys and surfer girls have all suddenly vacated the beach and many of the vehicles in the car park have left or are leaving. The last few have their doors flung open and a dozen surfers are hurriedly stowing their boards and stripping off wetsuits. They are actually *proper* surfing dudes, with long hair and beards, and bushy, bushy blonde hairdos and everything. They all make a big noise hooting at their remaining friends as they drive off, who in turn hoot back and cheer. There is a definite urgency about their departure. I don't know how surfing works, whether they're chasing the surf and racing across the peninsula to the other side or something... but to me the waves look eminently more surfy than they did before. Perhaps it's just that it's pub time now.

I once again drive along narrow, high-banked lanes. An impressive church tower comes into view on the outskirts of Saint David's, the gold on its clock face reflecting the sun. I realise this is not just a nice church, it's the cathedral, as I've just learnt that Saint David's is a city.

The road winds around and gets narrower and leads me to Saint Justinian, where there is very little at all. The tiny hamlet is named, as you'd expect, after Saint Justinian, who was a 6th-century holy man. Saint David was so impressed with Saint Justinian's holiness that he made him the Abbot of his cathedral, Saint David's – at Saint David's – so good they named him twice. In time, Justinian became disillusioned with the unholiness of the monks there and retreated to the sanctity of Ramsey Island, just over the water, where he set up a more devout community. Not all that devout though, because according to legend he was murdered by some of his own followers, who were getting tired of his strict ascetic ways, so they beheaded him. Justinian refused to stay after this, so he picked up his head and – it is said –

he crossed the sea – walking on the water – with his head under his arm. At some point he must have stopped walking, because he was buried on the mainland, in the remarkably intact, though roofless, white stone Saint Justinian's chapel, visible in a field just off the lane. His body was supposedly later removed and taken to Saint David's cathedral and interred alongside Saint David himself. Unfortunately for this story, the bones of Saints David and Justinian were carbon dated and shown to be from the 12th century or later, so six centuries after they were both believed to have lived. (Perhaps even Saints lie about their age.)

Steps at the end of the lane lead down towards a sheltered cove, where the old Lifeboat house is situated. This is much-photographed, and quite rightly so, because it's very picturesque: red with a slipway, facing Ramsey Sound and beyond that the rocks and peaks of Ramsey Island. This iconic old Lifeboat house is now somewhat marred by the new lifeboat station, built directly next to it. No disrespect to the new building, which is certainly impressive in its own way, but it doesn't have the character of its predecessor. A new, larger and improved boathouse was needed to house the Tamar-class Lifeboat, which was launched from the new station for the first time in 2016. More than 360 lives have so far been saved by these lifeboat stations.

The sun is sinking behind the highest peak of Ramsey Island and the wind is making an eerie noise on the telegraph wires. I drive a few hundred yards along the lane to a campsite I'd phoned earlier. There had been no answer, so I'd left a message, but no one got back to me. I drive onto the site and park up. To call it a campsite is flattering it really. A lot. It's just a field, but that's fine. A field which looks unkempt and abandoned. There are two other caravans in darkness, but no cars. There is an honesty box for your £4 per person per night fee. I get my diesel heater on, close the curtains and open a can of lager. It's a quiet evening. I'm in the middle of nowhere, with a view from the window of fields, low hedges, the lonely sea and a sky that goes on forever. I'm so tired, I sit and drink my can, thinking I won't physically be able to stay awake for much longer. After all, it's – I glance at my watch – approaching 5.30pm.

At 6pm, I look out of the window; it's completely dark. There's a moon, but it's now hidden behind clouds. There's nothing but darkness surrounding me. The only lights I can see are in the distance and rather than being a comfort, they only seem to illustrate how far away from everyone else I am. A light travels in an arc across the sky. It's like a searchlight or the Bat signal, but the fact that it happens three more times in close succession tells me it's the light signature for Strumble Head. An eight second pause, then four more sweeps. I can't see the lighthouse itself; like the mariners out in the dark ocean, I can only see its guiding light.

* * * * * * * * * *

I went to bed early - around ten. I didn't think I'd be able to get to sleep, but I drifted off straight away. I intended to get up very early to make the most of the daylight. I woke up at 4am. Too early. I woke up again at 6am. Too cold. I finally wake up at 8am. Too late!

I put the heater on and sit huddled in bed watching the

sunrise. The best bit is just before the sun breaks the horizon: gold and orange and deep purple. Once the sun has fully left the horizon the colour is gone and though the sun is still shining, it's rather dull and unspectacular.

In the cold morning light I drive the short distance into Saint David's. The cathedral bell is chiming as I arrive in the village. Town. I mean city. Yes, city. Saint David's is a city. Britain's smallest city. It was a city in the 16th century, but city status was lost in 1888, then restored in 1994, at the request of the Queen. I drive through it, not realising that's it. It really is little more than a village. It's also completely deserted. I thought on a Sunday it would be full of life, with people walking to church to the uplifting sound of the bells. Actually, the very few people I do see on my exploration are walking *away* from the cathedral. God only knows why.

The car park ticket machine doesn't have a fixed price, instead it has an optional donation, suggested price £1, which I think is brilliant value. You still need to buy a ticket, presumably you can put in however much money you want. (I opt for the suggested price. I don't imagine many people put in more.)

I walk back into the "city centre", passing a car sticker: SAVE THE MALES IN WALES. I'm not sure if it's a pun on SAVE THE WHALES or something else. (Turns out it's the strapline of a Welsh prostate cancer charity, which ties in neatly with my musings about Movember yesterday.)

Saint David's is so very quiet and so very closed. It seems to have completely shut down. Perhaps it's because it's the sabbath and no one works on the sabbath. We must assume working includes smiling, because the very few people I encounter are frowning with such gusto it looks like a full facial workout. An older couple pass me, faces pinched in the cold. They're wearing the same his 'n' hers puffa jackets, and they both have the same big, white, unisex hair. The only difference between them is that the man has a beard. I say a cheery "good morning"; she hesitates and then offers a monotone and grudging "hello", whilst he just ignores me.

I walk through back streets and narrow alleys and winding passages, passing little stone houses that look like a child's drawing, two windows, a door and a chimney. I hear the sound of a car and get excited because I think it might be someone else alive, but a woman just drives past me with the same dead, staring eyes.

The cathedral is very attractive. It isn't on the scale of finery as many other cathedrals, but it's a majestic building. The previous version was destroyed by Vikings and the current building was built by the Normans. Remember, it supposedly houses the bones of Saint David himself, the Patron Saint of Wales, who was born and brought up nearby and founded a monastery here. The city was of such historical religious importance that the Pope decreed that two pilgrimages to St David's were equivalent to one to Rome. It was visited by many pilgrims, including royalty, such as William, whose hobby was Conquering, which doesn't make him sound all that Christian. Or perhaps it does, when you consider that very popular church-sanctioned Mediaeval pastime, the Crusades.

Next to the cathedral are the ruins of the 13th-century

Bishop's Palace, an even more impressive building, now sadly a ruin: roofless, but the walls are in a very good state of preservation. There are Romanesque arches and the stonework is intricate and amazing.

A solitary seagull hovers in the grey air above the cathedral, silent and motionless, like an ornithological snapshot. It's quite unearthly, as though time has stopped. Which - I'm fairly sure - it hasn't.

I'm overjoyed when I spot a sign pointing to the refectory. I'm really cold and need some serious refection. When I get there I find the refectory is closed. The Bishop's Palace is closed. The cathedral gift shop is closed – not that I want a pencil sharpener with a bad picture of the cathedral on it. I wander back uphill through the town, passing the Ramsey Island Boat Trip office – which is closed. Nearby is an interesting looking espresso bar and I can hear music. Rock and roll music. I reach the door, where there is a closed sign. I get it – Saint David's is closed! As I'm turning away, a young man hurriedly pulls open the café door from the inside.

"Sorry…" he says with a smile, (A smile!) "Regardless of what it says on the door, we are actually open. Just."

Maybe there is a god! I look to the greying sky (I don't.) and thank Her. (I don't.) The café is upstairs amongst the rafters and exposed beams. It's comfortable and loungey. There's a "leaping hare" sculpture on display, which reminds me of something from *The Wicker Man*, which seems to be coming into my mind a lot at the moment. I'm the only customer, greatly outnumbered by the staff.

I have a lovely Americano and sit on a settee, trying to flick through a book on the St Davids (sic) Peninsula, but am constantly distracted by the conversation of the two junior staff, who busy themselves behind the counter. A young man in his twenties, who is regular staff and a girl in her late teens, who is a Saturday girl, or Sunday girl rather. She looks as cold as ice cream but still as sweet. He says something about David Grohl.

The girl frowns: "Who's he?"

"Who's he? Who's David Grohl?" Mouth agape. "*David Grohl!* He's from Nirvana."

"Oh."

"Don't you like Nirvana?"

"It's alright."

"*It's* alright?" Pause. "That is *not* the right answer!"

"I'm not really into music much."

"Oh… right." he says, then continues talking about every aspect of Nirvana while she gets on with filling the sugar basins. She is clearly yearning for the day she can leave and go to university.

I can appreciate where he's coming from. Nicky refuses to be drawn into a conversation about music. "I am not getting into a conversation about music." she'll say. If she ever hears a song and says: "I like this song." she will always quickly add: "And no, that's not an invitation to talk about music."

No one else comes into the café. I finish my coffee and leave the staff to their hormones and rather awkward, mis-matched flirting.

Outside in the cold, I have another lonely wander around the city of Saint David's. The high street is deserted still. The sun from the early morning is absent and instead it's overcast. Lamp posts are juddering in the wind. The hanging signs of closed inns are swinging. The shops are still shut and presumably aren't going to open now. Windows are dark and it's quite eerie. The *Sound Café* is silent. A shop called *Interesting Things* is closed and lacks interest. *The Veg Patch* says it's open, but it clearly isn't, the lights are off and there's no one inside. A bed and breakfast has an old fashioned *No Vacancies* sign in the window. The information centre has a distinct lack of information and its door is securely bolted.

I'm about to leave Saint David's, when I discover the visitor centre is open. And it's got a café. Which is open! I go in. As is the custom, I'm the only customer. I order a vegan breakfast from the friendly young serving man, who's so bored he's cleaning *the legs* of the chairs. I've never seen that done before.

"It's very quiet in the village... town... city."

He nods. "It's so quiet out of season and so few people live permanently in Pembrokeshire..." He sighs. "The city barely operates in the winter, but in season you can't move. You wouldn't get a seat in here or anywhere."

I want to see places out of season, but the downside is that the weather is bad and everywhere's closed.

While I'm eating, an old man comes in, with his even older mother. He's very tall; she's very small. In a booming, theatrical voice he orders: "A hot chocolate for mother, please, and a coffee for me."

The server scribbles down their order. "Would you like marshmallows with that?"

"She wouldn't, no, thank you."

The old lady leans forward. "What was that?"

In a loud, clear voice: "He asked if you would like marshmallows, mum. I said no, you wouldn't like marshmallows. You wouldn't, would you?"

She recoils. "Oh no... no."

"Would you like whipped cream on the hot chocolate?"

"No, mother wouldn't, thank you."

She raises her eyebrows expectantly. "What was that?"

"He asked if you'd like whipped cream, mum. I said no, you wouldn't."

She shudders. "Oh no... no."

Fortunately, there are no more questions, so they shuffle off to locate a table, only to find they're all but one vacant.

There are three staff at this point, one front of house and two chefs leaning idly on the counter. They all look exactly the same: short dark hair and neatly clipped beards. I had seen them all coming and going, but thought they were all the same person until this triple revelation. Anyway, the breakfast is gorgeous.

I've had a nice coffee, I've had a wonderful breakfast and I've spoken very briefly to some living people – and all of a sudden, the tiny city of Saint David's, with or without his apostrophe, seems a mighty fine little place and I would gladly do it again.

Feeling replete and resplendent, I leave my brand new friend, Saint David, and drop down into the village of Solva, which is yet another of those photogenic places that regularly appears on calendars and photographic books of scenic Wales. Admittedly, when it's modelling it's usually bathed in sunshine and looks beautiful; the creek is one of the most sheltered anchorages along this part of the coast and in season is lined with impressive and expensive yachts. On this occasion it isn't. There are currently very few boats moored in the creek. The sun has become just a white blur in the sky, lost behind a layer of cloud and the landscape is just pallid and grey.

I set off along a footpath which follows the edge of the creek, soon climbing uphill past a few isolated houses which have stunning views across the inlet and out towards the sea. On the tops, it's very windy. A little robin keeps flitting from branch to branch of the gorse and hawthorn bushes along the path, basically following me. It's very rough up here for such a frail-looking little bird. When I reach the very tip of the headland it starts raining, quite suddenly and quite heavily. My reliant robin abandons me and quickly disappears. I hastily make my way back along the path.

A couple are walking towards me, both wearing thick glasses. The girl approaches first with a dog, so I smile at the lovely dog and then have to follow it with a dutiful smile at her. The boy then gives me an Alpha-male grunt and stares at me hard through his lenses. He isn't very good at the Alpha male thing. He'd have been better weeing on her legs to mark his territory. I decide to leave Solva, before things turn nasty.

On the way to Haverfordwest, the sky is turning a very dark grey and it doesn't look like the rain has any plans of stopping any time soon. If ever.

I drive through the aptly named Newgale, where it's blowing a gale. Possibly a new one. It's a seaside place. On a blank noticeboard someone has penned, in thick black marker: JESUS SAVES, which is quite an odd graffito to find. Jesus may save, allegedly, but he seldom cleans off graffiti.

There are a few elderly couples sitting in their cars in the car park; all they can see is a steep bank of pebbles where the beach ought to be, a sea defence measure presumably. There is no glimpse of the beach or the sea, just a rising gradient of greys. If you like looking at banks of grey pebbles, then get along to Newgale car park. In the rain it looks very dismal. #1

I pass a pub that serves GREAT FOOD AND REAL ALES. So the food is great but might not be real, whereas the ales are real but might not be great. (I know I'm pedantic, but it gets me through the day.)

Haverfordwest is a market town and the county town

of Pembrokeshire. I spend a good five minutes driving around the streets, turning down every intriguing little side street, up steep inclines, round tight corners. It looks quirky and full of character, full of attractive old buildings, colourful terrace rows with a nice church at a high point overlooking the town; the only problem is that at this moment I've had my fill of walking around towns in the rain, a town which appears predominantly closed, so for me it's a driving tour only and I move on.

* * * * * * * * * *

It's relatively flat as I drive towards another peninsula. The fields have become very large and open and there are very few trees. The tallest thing here is a line of telegraph poles, which disappear into the distance.

I pull into the car park in Dale, where the couple I met on Ynys Dinas had recommended I stay the night. There are signs EVERYWHERE warning me not to stay the night or I'll definitely and absolutely be prosecuted without further ado, which is very disappointing – and also not, because for me Dale is a fail. The couple had built Dale up to be a paradise and that can only lead to disappointment. What I find is a rather nondescript little village which feels a bit odd. And deserted. And sort of nothing. It feels like it's just some houses in the rain. Sorry Dale. I think the rain and my mood have a lot to do with it, but the views across the sea to the multiple chimneys of Milford Haven also don't help. #2

I drive through the village and follow the dead-end road towards the Saint Ann's headland. A flock of black birds take off in front of me, looking surreal and very false. I park in a National Trust car park and walk the rest of the way along the dead-end lane. It's windy, cold and wet. I have a look at the current and former lighthouses and then head back to the van. I don't get the best feelings from Saint Ann's Head, but I can't really say why, apart from perhaps the ever-present view of the industrialised Milford Haven over the water, which ruins the aspect and the atmosphere.

I arrived in the rain and I leave in the rain. End of.

* * * * * * * * * * *

If Brendan was with me…

Brendan would have enjoyed the various cafes and pubs that I went in, not that they would necessarily have enjoyed him, and probably not all would have been dog-friendly. But then he isn't always a friendly dog. He would have barked incessantly at the surfers. They would have infuriated him. They're people and they're carrying things and they aren't normally there; it would be like a hatrick of fury. Furry fury. But apart from that I would have loved having him on board, because I love his pet sounds and his funny ways.

NOTES

#1: Just to put the record straight, when I later Google Newgale, it looks lovely in the sunshine.

#2: Likewise, to be fair to Dale, after Googling it later, it looks better in the sun, but no amount of sunshine can alter the fact that it has a view of Milford Haven.

ABOVE and BELOW: Whitesands Bay, Pembrokeshire.

CHAPTER 11: SOCIETAL MALAISE

In which Eagle One gets grounded, a pub landlord has a bath. I stroll on a military target range and witness the dystopian inspiration for the sci-fi classic *Blade Runner*.

From Saint Ann's Head to Pembroke, as the crow flies, shouldn't be that difficult. It really shouldn't. However, Satnav Sally is taking me on a really random and pointless wild goose chase and a half. (No gooses were harmed in this narrative.) At one point we do five consecutive lefts – surely that means we've gone round in a circle or square or tetrahedron or something?

We cross a toll bridge; I don't realise until all the traffic is stopping and the drivers in front start handing money over. At first, I think it's a very polite and organised mugging. The man in the toll booth just vacantly, silently holds out his hand. I'm not even sure his eyes are open. I ask how much it is. He very slowly leans forward, looks over my van in deep consternation, then sinks back and says with a low sigh: "Go on… seventy-five pence then." as though he's doing me a favour. I hand him the correct change. "Merry Christmas." he says, slow and deadpan.

I return the rather premature greeting and drive on, feeling that I've just been insulted somehow.

Surprisingly, Milford Haven looks very nice close-up. It's completely dark as I pass through and I'm guessing that's the best way to see it. It's just a jungle of white lights, which actually look quite festive, though admittedly that isn't part of the design. I drive through Pembroke and that too is decked out with Christmas lights, but these are intentional. The little I see of Pembroke looks impressive enough.

The last stretch of the journey is back out into the countryside, to a campsite at an inn. I had booked by phone and the chap had warned me most apologetically that the grass hadn't been cut and was ankle high. I had laughed and said it wouldn't be a problem and anyway I preferred natural grass. He sounded genuinely upset as he told me someone had complained about it recently and it was their only ever complaint. I felt quite sorry for him.

I see the pub ahead, a shining beacon in the darkness.

"Turn left at the pub," he'd said, "then bear right after the car park. I'll leave the gate open, so you can't go wrong." What he *actually* meant was: "I *won't* leave the gate open for you, I'll go and have a bath instead."

I turn left at the pub, then right after the car park, then I come to a closed gate, so I assume I'm in the wrong place, but on the other side of the gate – the *closed* gate – is a field with caravans in it, so it must be right. This isn't a huge issue, the gate isn't locked, so I open it and drive in.

"Once through the *open gate*," he'd said, "Take a sharp left and then park up." What he actually meant was: "If you take a sharp left your van will definitely get bogged down. I'll probably hear your wheels spinning, as long as I'm not running the hot tap... because I'll be in the bath."

I try to follow his instructions, but get stuck because the grass is so long, *too long,* folded over and water-logged. The wheels are spinning and sinking. It takes some manoeuvring to get Eagle One free. I try to find another spot to park.

"I'll come over when I see you pull in." he'd said. What he actually meant was: "I *won't* come over when you pull in. I'll still be in the bath."

I can't find the electric hook-up, which he'd said would be there. I trail a familiar orange wire – the colour of electric hook-up cables – but it disappears into the long grass and seems to go underground. I give up looking and go into the pub.

True to form, I seem to be the only customer. It feels a few degrees colder inside the pub than outside, but that might partly be the atmosphere. It's not very inviting. At all. I stand at the empty bar and wait. Then I wait a bit more. I look around for a bell or some other signalling device, but there isn't one. After a few minutes I hear slow, heavy footsteps slumping towards me from a long way off. A young woman appears.

"Hi." I say. "I spoke to someone earlier and booked on the campsite."

"Was it dad?"

I look at her for a moment. "I don't know. It was a man."

"Yes, it will have been dad then."

I detect a West Country accent. I wonder just how far I've driven in the dark. "Dad's in the bath at the moment. I'll tell him you're here."

She goes upstairs to tell Dad. I hear her slow, laboured footsteps on bare, creaking wooden stairs. I do some more waiting. The pub is cold and drab and badly lit. The footsteps on the stairs start again, getting slowly but steadily nearer. She reappears and wipes her brow; she looks exhausted.

"He'll be about ten minutes, then he'll sort you out."

I order a pint and sit down to wait. On my own. Twenty minutes pass. No one shows. There's no sign of Dad, who presumably remains upstairs, up to his neck in suds. Half an hour passes. If I'd known it was bath night I wouldn't have come.

The girl keeps coming to apologise and heaving herself back up the bare wooden stairs to check on Dad's progress and apologising more profusely each time she reappears. After forty minutes I notice her through the window, walking around the campsite with a torch. She comes wearily back inside. She can't work out where the wire goes either. She phones her brother, but he doesn't know. She apologises again for Dad's tardiness. I give up waiting for Dad in his luxury bath; I thank her for her help and say I'll go back to the site and try again myself.

Scrabbling around in the darkness and the incredibly long grass, I eventually manage to find the power cable; the grass has grown around it, effectively burying it. With brute force I'm able to pull it free and follow it to a junction box – also buried in the grass – and plug in. I'm on the grid!

I've paid a tenner for this rather scruffy site. It looks like a traveller encampment and I'm not impressed. There are a few ramshackle caravans, but they're dark and I don't think anyone has been in them for some time. They actually look abandoned. I'm regretting coming here. Ten pounds for this dump is not in any way good value.

An older man with a grey beard, a wide-brimmed hat and glasses suddenly appears and greets me cheerfully. "Hello there! Oh, have you sorted it?"

"Just!" I say triumphantly. "Sorry to disturb your bath."

He smiles and seems a little embarrassed. He takes a look at the wire and junction box configuration.

"Know all about electrics." he says. He sounds like a cowboy. I wonder if it's the hat. Or whether he's *trying* to sound like a cowboy. A Welsh cowboy. "Understand them 'cause I work in television." It seems an odd thing for a pub landlord to say, but I let it go. He looks over Eagle One and we chat for a while about camper vans. He points at the pub car park, where I expect to see he's parked his horse. There's no horse. "That's mine there."

"Your what?"

"Van.My van. Beautiful." There's no van either. Not that I can see anyway. The car park appears to be empty. I nod politely. The conversation is very odd and we both seem to be getting more and more confused, until he says suddenly: "I'm local."

I frown. "Well… yeah." Presumably he lives in the pub.

"I live down the road."

"Not in the pub?"

"No… no. That's what I'm saying… I'm *a* local…"

"Erm… OK."

"This is my local… My local pub. I was in the pub playing snooker. In the back room. When you came in. I just came out to help."

All the pieces fall into place. "Oh… so you're *not* Dad? The landlord, I mean."

He laughs. "No… no. Oh god no! *No!* I wondered why you mentioned the bath! No… Geoff hasn't surfaced yet. No, no, no… Geoff's *much* bigger than me! Oh my god… Geoff's a… a *big* man… Very big… Much, *much,* considerably bigger than me."

We both laugh. Perhaps we laugh a bit too much. It all seems so confusing and surreal here. I thank him profusely for his strange kindness and he wanders off through the darkness, back towards his invisible van and the overly-bright unbeckoning lights of the pub.

* * * * * * * * * * *

It's very windy in the night. Eagle One rocks from side to side and I don't sleep very well at all. As a result, I have a bit of a lazier morning, but am ready to leave at ten. I step out of the van to unplug the troublesome electric hook-up lead and my heart sinks. Eagle One has a flat tyre. I instantly know it happened on the rutted gravel driveway last night as I drove in. There had been a lurch and an odd noise, but I had assumed it was just a loose stone under the tyres. To make matters worse, I haven't got round to replacing the damaged spare since the blow out.

I phone the AA, but am immediately told that one of their conditions of service is that the vehicle carries a usable spare. They don't carry spare tyres, so the best they can do is to contact local garages until they've found one that has the correct tyre, but the tyres and the call out charge will be down to me. I have no choice but to accept.

It's over an hour before the mechanic arrives. Ewan is very friendly and helpful. I buy two new tyres, thus replacing the spare as well, so now Eagle One is fully functioning again. Ewan finds a large steel screw in the tyre. In daylight when I look around the site... or rather the *sight*... the grass is covered with odd bits of metal and old junk, so before long something was bound to happen to someone. It's a mess. It looks like an old scrapyard. I walk over to the pub to complain, but the pub is closed. I don't believe they haven't seen I'm still there, way after checking out time and that a breakdown vehicle has arrived. I also don't believe they're all out. Maybe Geoff's still in the bath. Their dogs are certainly in, but don't answer the door.

The night on that tatty, scruffy, badly-run site has cost me in excess of three hundred quid. Because Ewan is so helpful and gives me some advice about other issues with my van, he earns himself a ten pound tip. It's worth it to get me back on the road. By now though, it's early afternoon and I've lost the majority of the daylight. I could be very pissed off, but I'm just glad to be mobile again.

I pass the pub as I leave. That landlord never did show. For all I know he might have died in that bath. #1

* * * * * * * * * * *

I drive to the coast at the south end of the Pembroke peninsula. I want to see a little chapel built half way down a cliff, but you have to cross a danger area, namely Castlemartin Artillery Testing Range. You aren't allowed to pass if there's a red flag flying. There's a gate, which is open, and a flagpole and I can see the red flag is furled around the base, so I assume it's clear to enter. I follow the winding lane between large, rough, open fields. There are occasionally other turnings and driveways, barred by locked gates at which there are red flags flapping violently, their edges shredded from the constant salt wind. The red contrasts with the watery grey of the sky, in an otherwise monochrome landscape.

A very ragged seagull glides across the sky; he looks like he's been repeatedly blown up. Perhaps he has. There are ruined buildings dotted about and I'm pretty sure I can see some tanks on the horizon. At the end of the lane there's a small car park. I pull on the handbrake and notice a sinister man with binoculars is staring at me, which really makes me feel that I shouldn't be here. He's definitely watching me. And he's making a point of being obvious about it. The big giveaway is that he's only about ten yards away.

It's very cold as I step out onto the tarmac. There's a light sea mist hanging in the air and occasional ferocious spasms of rain. The binocular man, clad in heavy waterproofs, has me in his sights as I follow a set of stone steps downhill towards the tiny Saint Govan's chapel. I'm surprised to hear sudden voices, seemingly coming from nowhere and a woman appears from the hidden chapel entrance. She hasn't seen me, as she's focusing on the steps as she ascends. I don't want her to be startled when she looks up and I'm standing there, so I call out a tentative "Hello!" This has the opposite effect to my intention and she screams. She clasps a hand to her mouth and stares, then her shoulders relax and she drops her hand: she has obviously decided I'm not going to kill her. She starts laughing in embarrassment. "Oh, I didn't see you there." Her husband appears behind her, looks at her and rolls his eyes. Perhaps this happens a lot.

She looks me up and down. "Well," she says, "It could be Saint Govan himself." Probably because I have my hood up. I wish I'd said "Bless you my child." or something else ecclesiastical, but I don't; I'm still trying to convince her that I'm not going to kill her. I smile politely.

They're a nice, friendly older couple. They confirm the man with the binoculars is the security guard for the artillery range and he's a stickler for doing his job. He has binoculars and he's damn well going to use them. The old chap says the tanks I thought I'd seen are dummy tanks for target practise. They say goodbye, climb the steps and a few minutes later I hear their car departing and I'm alone, just me, the harsh wind, the rain, the ragged seagull and the waterproof man with binoculars.

I duck down through the low doorway and enter the simple cell-like room of Saint Govan's chapel. It has an arched ceiling and thick walls, with occasional glassless windows, which look out over the sea and a cliff stack in a little cove below. I came here as a child, I'm almost certain. I have vivid memories of it, which is odd, because it isn't the sort of place my mum and dad would be interested in and it's not the sort of place you bring children, but I remember it distinctly.

It's a lovely, atmospheric place to be alone on a bad day, but it's very cold and funnelling the wind. I sit there for as long as I can, trying to think profound thoughts, like "If I could have any cake in the world right now, what would I choose?" I can't arrive at a satisfactory answer, so I return to Eagle One and head back along the driveway. There's no sign of binocular man now. There's no sign of anyone, but the shredded red flags keep flapping.

* * * * * * * * * *

Around the coastal lanes there is very little traffic and I'm driving slowly, just enjoying the landscape. Every view in every direction is worthy of being put on a calendar. I'm heading towards Penfro, (Pembroke town) via a meandering, circuitous route. The light is fading already.

Pembroke ("[The] County Council make Pembrokeshire a terrible place to live", "the drivers are crap they park where the fucking like" (sic), "Lack off gorgeous ladies" (sic), "Lack of work") was obviously the original county town of Pembrokeshire, but not now. Now it's, bizarrely, Haverfordwest. I drive twice round Pembroke town in the last of the daylight and don't know whether I'm going to stop, because nothing really grabs me. It's an attractive enough town, the main street – cunningly called Main Street – is not unpleasant. I *do* stop, because I feel I *ought to*, rather than I *want to*, and thinking that on foot I might discover the secrets of the town. The Norman castle is justly famous, of course. It was the birthplace of King Henry VII, who became the first Tudor king after he defeated Richard III at the Battle of Bosworth Field. That decisive battle effectively ended the War of the Roses. Henry VII was Henry VIII's dad. Henry VIII is considerably more famous, considerably more corpulent and had considerably more wives.

The streets of Pembroke are fairly quiet, but still it's a bustling metropolis compared to the City of Saint David. I stroll about, but no pub or café really grabs me. It's almost dark and the roads suddenly seem to get busy as people start to head home and the shop keepers are starting to pack away their wares. Pembroke feels like a town winding down.

I join the throng of homeward vehicles and drive a few miles to my site for the night in a tiny village just outside Pembroke, right next to a little church. I'm the only person on the site and the church tower looms over my van. The facilities are very basic – I mean army basic. That doesn't generally bother me, as long as it's reflected in the price. It's a very nice spot, ie. it doesn't look like the set of Steptoe and Son like last night's site, though it's nearly double the price – excluding van repairs, call out charges and tips.

Anyway, I'm paying all this money so I have to give the showers a go. I assume they probably won't be as bad as they look at first glance... But I'm wrong. They're worse. They're full of cobwebs and dead insects, but I get by. Walking back across the deserted site towards Eagle One, the church is very spooky in the crescent moonlight. There's so little light pollution in the area and a clear sky, so the heavens look like a dazzling Jackson Pollock; tiny suns sprayed across the impenetrably blackness of space, the final frontier.

Curtains closed, heater on, bed made up, sleep. Goodnight.

* * * * * * * * * * *

Curtains open, heater on, bed away, wide awake. Good morning.

I drive eastwards on this fine, sunny day. I seem to be driving away from the sun and towards very dark grey skies and a very vivid rainbow. Then the rain comes. So, I drive eastwards through the driving rain. Eagle One has begun having those acceleration problems again, with a loss of power on gradients, which implies it might be dampness related, because it hasn't occurred in the sunny weather.

I follow Satnav Sally's instructions and end up in a retail

park. Anyone who knows me at all knows that's the *very last* place I'd ever want to be. It's a hot off the press, paint still wet, newly built retail park with most of the units still unoccupied and everything covered with a thick layer of concrete dust. I decide to take a break; there's a brand new Costa drive-through, which I'd use except it has a height barrier, so I buy a takeaway americano from the café, I'd normally sit inside, but I find the place rather soulless, especially the views from the windows. I'd rather sit in my van, though the views are exactly the same actually, as glass doesn't contain magical properties – as far as I know – but at least I'm comfortable in my familiar surroundings.

Suitably caffeine-fuelled, we crawl through Swansea to the interesting little district of Mumbles. Mumbles is a jumble of fascinating cafés, bistros, bars, pubs, inns and so forth. It's situated on the western shore of Swansea Bay, with views across to Port Talbot. Unfortunately.

It's stopped raining and the sun's come out again. Looking across the bay, it isn't the best view, but it never is when you're looking at an urban or industrial area. Or both. But in the background there are rolling green hills.

I wander along the seafront. A solitary seagull perches on the apex of the RNLI office, crying his cry unchallenged. The nearby pier is late Victorian and its ironwork is unusually ornate. A new lifeboat boathouse has recently been installed at the end of the pier. This is happening everywhere now, such as Saint Justinian and Llandudno; the new Tamar class lifeboats are too big for most of the old boathouses, so every station is having to erect a larger one. In 1947, while attempting a rescue, every man of the crew was tragically lost.

On one side of the pier stands the quaint old RNLI boathouse, now an attractive relic. On the other side is the octagonal tower of Mumbles lighthouse, still operational, standing on an island off Mumbles Head. It's the most photographed structure in the area.

* * * * * * * * * * *

Dark clouds, heavy with rain, are starting to gather as I leave Mumbles. I try to boost Eagle One up with the gift of some cheap fuel: the cheapest yet. From an independent garage, so fuel *and* karma, but it doesn't seem to help her to go any faster.

I drive through the busy main roads of Swansea. Standing proudly above the other buildings is a gleaming white art deco clock tower, actually part of the Guildhall, which opened in the 'Thirties. The design caused controversy at the time, being art deco, which was often considered to be brash, vulgar and in very bad taste. Today, it stands out as a striking landmark with its distinctive forty-eight metre clocktower, which includes the prow of a Viking longboat, in honour of Sweyn Forkbeard, who is credited as the founder of Swansea.

I pass a Ferris wheel then small guesthouses and hotels. Crossing over the river Tawe – the Welsh name for Swansea is Abertawe – and a marina, full of lovely boats. A miniature corner pub, the *Swansea Jack*, is closed, boarded up, for sale by auction. In the distance, there are the green hills, but lined with pylons and wind turbines.

As the main road splits into lanes, one of the lanes

is labelled "Amazon", which I think is a most un-Welsh sounding place name. Then I see the huge pre-fab warehouses and realise it refers to Amazon, as in *Amazon*, as in Amazon UK, the massive online retailer. It's so huge it has its own road markings.

Leaving Swansea, the M4 motorway is raised on huge, concrete stilts. It snakes above an alien cityscape, above the roofs and chimneys of a dystopian paradigm. Or Port Talbot, as it's also known. It's a bizarre creation, like something from *Charlie and the Chocolate Factory*, or the *Mouse Trap* game, or a Rube Goldberg machine. It's all funnels and twisting, curling pipes and plumes of smoke, rising and billowing like mushroom clouds. It looks surreal and demonic; more dark and satanic than any mill William Blake ever perambulated adjacent to. These are the blast furnaces at Port Talbot steelworks.

English film director and producer, Sir Ridley Scott, is quoted as saying that the sight of Port Talbot at night provided the inspiration for his vision of a dystopian near-future in the neo-noir epic *Blade Runner*. The 1982 film was adapted from Philip K. Dick's sci-fi novel *Do Androids Dream of Electric Sheep?* (They don't.) Upon release, the film was commercially a dud, though it has gone on to be hailed as a classic.

Despite being one of the largest steelworks in the world, the future of Port Talbot has long been under threat. If the plant closes, a *huge* section of the townspeople will lose their jobs, because - despite its demonic countenance and dystopian image - the works is the lifeblood of the area.

The town is said to be the most polluted place in

Wales and the most polluted in the United Kingdom outside London. It is often referred to as *Port Toilet*. The steelworks owns the largest privately-owned beach in Europe, but it's filthy and unfit to use. The company has recently been bought out by an Indian firm and there are plans to make Port Talbot into "a garden with a steelworks in it". That can only be a good thing.

I drive along the heartless, soulless, dystopian, raised concrete highway and leave the fascinating, unmistakeable, inspirational Port Talbot behind, in its haze of smoke, steam and fumes.

I pass through the outskirts of Bridgend, a former market town. Despite the sinister associations that have been attached to it, mainly via the tabloid press, it looks like anywhere else I've driven through. Between January 2007 and February 2009, 26 people killed themselves within Bridgend county. Many were between the ages of 13 and 17 and all but one died from hanging. It was speculated that a "suicide cult" was to blame. Though police found no evidence of such, many of the victims knew each other. The media have been blamed for their melodramatic and exaggerated way of reporting, and sometimes misrepresenting or misunderstanding statistics.

A documentary was made in 2013 and a film drama in 2015, both imaginatively titled *Bridgend*. The drama in particular has been highly criticised as being "sensationalist, exploitative and lacking truth" with a huge amount of artistic license being taken with gratuitous scenes. For example, the strapline used on the film posters was: YOU WILL NEVER LEAVE, which is almost identical to the town signs for Royston Vasey in the *League of Gentlemen*, ("YOU'LL NEVER LEAVE") from sixteen years earlier.

The locals blamed drink, drugs and boredom; they said there was nothing for teenagers to do, except get drunk, take drugs and find an easy way out. According to a spokesman from the local Samaritans, it wasn't headline news after the first few young men had died, but when the first young woman had hanged herself, there was a front-page media frenzy.

I watched the documentary, which was interesting, but I found it quite gratuitous, insensitive and intrusive. There were painfully long shots of people's emotion and grief, which lingered *far* too long to be acceptable. The film maker narrated it himself; unfortunately, he sounded insincere, overly-dramatic and sensational, which made the whole thing sound like a spoof.

There has been talk of devil worship, serial killers, internet cults and suicide pacts. There is no evidence of any of these. Instead it looks like the regularity of the suicides has desensitized people, and made suicide look like a viable way out. The suicides are very likely "a symptom of a deeper societal malaise." Everywhere there are symptoms of "societal malaise". That's the society we've created.

* * * * * * * * * * *

I had booked a campsite at the oddly named Llantwit Major. The old part of town is lovely: whitewashed stone and small, ancient buildings. The new part is functional. I check in at the site, which is again expensive, but at least the facilities are first class, then I set off lighthouse hunting.

I arrive at the Nash Head cliff top car park. There are two lighthouses here, one no longer active, with its lantern section removed. I always think this is undignified for a lighthouse. It wouldn't be too bad if there wasn't a fully functioning version within the same complex, standing proudly, fully erect and flashing at all and sundry. Conveniently, a public footpath leads right through the lighthouse compound, with its various outbuildings, fog signal, cottages and stores.

I got here just in time for the sunset, though it isn't spectacular. But the sun does indeed set. Banks of white billowing clouds gather on the horizon over the sea. The land gets darker, but the sky is still bright. It suddenly goes bitterly cold. There's a slow, solemn bell tolling a lonely lament, which I think is coming from a buoy in the sea; it reminds me of that legend of the undersea kingdom. I feel a bit poignant, as I often do in the dwindling light, with the sombre tolling and an uninterrupted view over the sea towards the streak of light on the horizon.

It's funny how I've adjusted and synched almost with the daylight. It feels late in the evening now: late, mysterious and quiet. But for most people, it's actually only the end of the working day. For them it's the start of the evening, the start of their own time. By the time I arrive back at the site, it's completely dark and feels very late, but it's barely 7pm.

* * * * * * * * * * *

<u>If Brendan was with me...</u>

He would have gone mad when the kindly Welsh cowboy approached the van to help with the electrics. He wouldn't have liked the artillery testing range at all and would have spotted the man with binoculars straight away and tried to neutralise him. He wouldn't have liked the little chapel - it has no TV and is breezy - but he might possibly have tolerated the evening lighthouse walk.

ABOVE: Stormclouds on the open road.

ABOVE: Stunning Rhossili beach, South Wales.

NOTES

#1: I probably shouldn't be surprised to learn that the pub in question stopped trading not long after my visit. The business had been run into the ground and the building badly neglected. It has since been bought and refurbished - it now looks quite stunning. I wish it well.

CHAPTER 12: THE DEEP SOUTH (OF WALES)

In which I visit *Gavin and Stacey* country and *Doctor Who* land and walk on Fred West's grave. I visit the Severn Bridge, a well-known suicide blackspot, and I think I've found a dead body. Things get Manic and finally come to a sticky end.

I open the curtains to a lovely sunny morning. According to Nicky it's going to be sunny here all day. People are going about their business, happily strolling towards the shower block with a towel over the shoulder or strolling back from the shop with a newspaper under the arm. There's a lot of strolling going on. This site has a lot going for it, including a shop, café and a children's play area with little pedal cars. (I was asked to get off them though.)

Today, along with the sunshine, I'm going to Barry Island, famously where *Gavin and Stacey* was filmed. Tidy. I'm currently listening to the Manic Street Preachers - as we're approaching their region of Wales - and they're desperately trying to apprise me of their design for life.

Ynys Barri. Or often Ynys y Barri. Either way, Barry Island. As you'd expect, Barry Island was originally an island, until the late Victorian era when it was attached to the mainland via a road bridge.

I try to park in a car park, which has temporary wire fencing around it. There are a couple of cars there and a few vans. The ticket machine is covered over. When I look up there are two dozen men in hard hats staring at me from scaffolding, wondering why I'm driving round their cars and vans, when it should be obvious that the car park's closed and any day it will be dug up and filled with the foundations of new homes. None of the hard-hatters speak. No one comes over to say "It's closed. You can't park here." No one turns to their colleague and says "Look at this idiot, what does he think he's doing?" No one says or does anything – they just stand there impassively, which is somehow much, much worse than any of the above. It's very disconcerting. Because they've unsettled me, I drive around the near-empty car park three times. I'm sure it doesn't say closed anywhere. I look around again. It *definitely* doesn't say closed. Maybe it's still open. I don't know… but I'm too embarrassed to stop here now, so I drive off – very slowly as though I *want* to drive off and I'm going in my own good time.

Embarrassment's a funny old thing. Or not. I'm not sure what – in evolutionary terms – it's actually for. If we fall over and hurt ourselves, the first thing we do is bounce up again, refuse help, say we're fine and walk away trying hard not to limp, cry or call for an air ambulance until we've turned the corner.

Well, I'm embarrassed and it isn't getting any better. There's no way out the way I'd come in, so I follow an exit road, but this leads to an estate of modern but tasteful newbuild houses – houses that the same workmen had probably erected a few weeks before. Probably on another car park. Every road I turn down is a dead end; I try the next one and repeat. Another dead end. I'm driving faster and more desperately. The workmen must be standing on their scaffolding, watching bemused as my van keeps appearing and disappearing down different streets. I seem to be trapped on this estate. There doesn't seem to be a way out... except through that car park. And that's not going to happen.

My embarrassment is going critical; it's off the scale at the red end. I'm wondering whether the easiest option might be to park up and wait until nightfall then sneak out under cover of darkness. At that moment a car appears, bumping along one of the untarmacked roads, being driven with confidence; this is someone who knows where they're going, knows the way out of this housing labyrinth. I hit the accelerator and speed off at 20mph, trundling after them, hoping they aren't just going home with their shopping. Because if they are I'm coming with them. But my hunch is right, following the car I find freedom, off the estate and back onto a main road. Yes!

If something similar happens to you, my advice is: firstly, don't panic. If worst comes to worst, as it so often does, if you can spot a street name you can call for a taxi and then follow it out of the maze. Alternatively, to save further embarrassment, you can abandon your car, get *into* the taxi and drive off, then sell your vehicle later on eBay.

I manage to find parking on a street where there's no scaffolding, no workmen and no charge. I'm not gonna lie to you, it's right on the seafront, so all in all a much better spot, though it stinks of greasy fried bacon. There are a few people sitting outside a café, because it's sunny, regardless of the bitter cold. It turns out to be Marco's Café, which featured in Gavin and Stacey series 3, where Stacey worked.

I walk along the fine, sandy beach. In 1995, serial killer, Fred West, had his ashes scattered here. But don't let's dwell on that. The bay is proper lush, contained between two small, grassy headlands. There's the constant call of seabirds, competing with a wailing siren in the distance, but growing nearer.

The sand is soft and clean, apart from Fred West's ashes, and the sea is sparkling in the sunshine. The beach is full of dogs taking their people for a walk. Three spritely pensioners pass me doing Nordic walking: walking with two poles, though why walking with *Poles* makes it *Nordic* I don't know. It looks incredibly silly on flat land, such as a beach or a park, but apparently it burns twice the calories.

I do like the look of beach huts. There is a row of them along one side of the promenade. I like the fact they're traditional and colourful and just sum up the seaside. Unfortunately, on closer inspection these are rather tacky, multicoloured and pre-fabricated, so they have a look of the Portaloo about them. Nearby are the public toilets, so I whizz in briefly. The washbasins are those automatic ones where you put your hands in a recess and it squirts liquid soap at you, then water, but not enough, then the dryer comes on, but globs of soap and drops of water keep dropping on you, then the dryer stops and you can't reactivate it without going through the whole process again, so you give up and leave with wet, sticky, foaming hands. I leave with wet, sticky, foaming hands.

A path leads from the prom around the grassy headland known as Nell's Point, where there are the remains of a coastal searchlight placement. In the 'Sixties, the site was developed by Billy Butlin, who built his last and smallest holiday camp here. It was hugely successful until the 1980s, when its fortunes began to fade. Perhaps because the New Romantics spent too long in their chalets doing their hair. It closed in 1986, when the Doctor Who crew briefly moved onto the derelict site to film the seventh Doctor story *Delta and the Bannermen*, which featured a cast of well-known and talented actors, as well as Bonnie Langford. The camp later re-opened with a new owner, but finally closed for good a decade later. It was demolished to make way for a housing estate.

I pass a building resembling a coastguard lookout station, which is in fact a National Coastwatch Institute lookout. The various stations are manned by volunteers, who look out to sea to try and spot people in need of assistance. The NCI was set up on the Lizard, Cornwall in 1994, following a double drowning close to a recently closed coastguard station. There are now several dozen stations across England and Wales, with over 2000 volunteers. Their strapline is "Eyes on the coast, looking out for you."

Heading back towards the centre of the prom, I pass the funfare, which is very colourful and clean, but all the rides are standing still and it's presumably closed for the season. John's Café is shuttered. Jeff's Ice Cream is shuttered. But Coffee Cove is open! Coastal Coffee is open! Harbour Amusements is open! So, we might conclude from this that tying your business name in with the beach or seaside must be good for trade, whereas using your own name isn't. So, Dennis's Pants – if it existed – would most probably be closed, whereas Seaside Slacks would possibly be open.

Sitting in a comfortable, if ostentatious, winged chair in a cafe, I drink a lovely strong coffee and read a local magazine about the Cardiff music and arts scene, which I pick up solely because it has a photo of Blondie on the cover. Looking out of the window at the beach and the sea, I'm pleasantly surprised by Barry Island. If it has fallen on hard times, and I'm sure it must have done, as most seaside places have, then there's very little evidence, because it looks well-kempt, freshly painted, clean and bright. It doesn't look in any way as though it's neglected or gone to seed. Efforts have been made to put up information boards along the seafront and the headland about the history of the places and the views, and there are pieces of art everywhere. Much of the art says BARRY ISLAND in big letters, in case you forget where you are, but it sounds like a town that's proud of what it is and wants to shout its name loud – and in capitals – and I can't knock it for that.

Oh! I'm not gonna lie to you, I'm proper sorry to leave Barry Island as I've had a really lush time. It's been tidy. The only reason I don't stay longer, is because I want to leave on a high. I don't want to stumble across all Barry's grotty bits. Maybe I've merely been lucky and I've just, by chance, stumbled across all the good parts... I'm sure it has its bad parts as well. Show me the good in any town and I'll show you the bad. That makes me sound like the negative one, sitting here with my glass half empty... So why don't *you* show me the bad in any town and *I'll* show you the good.

Seemingly, Barry doesn't want to let me leave. By following SatNav Sally's advice, I end up staying much longer than I intend to, driving up and down every street Barry owns. I can honestly say I still haven't seen a bad bit. By ignoring her advice, I eventually manage to find a way out of town.

* * * * * * * * * * *

It all looks very pleasantly suburban as I approach Penarth. I park up and walk along the promenade, which has a number of cafes and restaurants, most having tables outside facing the shore. The best feature of Penarth is surely the late-Victorian pier, which is one of the most picturesque piers I've ever walked upon. The art deco Pavilion was added in 1930; it currently houses an art gallery and café, which is lovely, warm, tastefully decorated and has views across the bay. The coffee, unfortunately, is rank. It's like old fashioned filter coffee that's been sitting in its glass pot since a week last Friday. It's bitter and vile. Tastes differ, obviously, and I like what I like. To me, this is *evil* and I leave it. Bad, *bad* coffee!

I decide to walk into Cardiff Bay along the Wales Coastal Path. I follow the signs steeply uphill, through a park only to find it blocked off at the top because the path has fallen into the sea. It would be helpful if they'd put a sign at the bottom of all the steps I've just walked up. There's no diversion offered, just a closed sign and a big wire fence. I don't know the way into Cardiff on foot, so I decide to abort and have a look around Penarth town centre instead. A clothes shop is having a sale and everything must go. Cafes are full of smiling, chatting elderly people. It looks like a very genteel, well-to-do country town. You could describe it as "charming", if you wanted to.

I queue up in the Co-op – which admittedly is not exclusive to country towns – to buy a rhubarb pie. There's an old lady in front of me, who's looking very furtive, eyeing the liquor cabinet behind the till.

"It's not for me...." she says earnestly to the shop assistant, "but how much is a bottle of vodka? *It's not for me.*"

The shop assistant begins patiently talking her through the various sizes and prices on offer, which vary greatly.

The old lady's grey, wiry eyebrows rise, aghast. "*How much*? It's not for me. I don't drink. No, a bigger bottle than that... No, cheaper than that. A bigger bottle but for less money."

All the while, the queue at the till is mounting. In the time I've been waiting, my rhubarb pie has gone past its sell-by date. The shop assistant makes an announcement for extra help on the tills and takes a deep breath then smiles politely and with renewed patience at the old lady.

"As I say, it's not for me. Oh, I don't know now... There's too much choice... Could you write the prices down for me?"

The shop assistant very obligingly jots a few brands and prices down, then straightens up, smiles again and holds the scribbled note out to the old lady, who doesn't even glance at it. "Actually, forget it for now…" She waves a hand dismissively at the list. "I'll call back tomorrow when I've got more time." She turns away but swings round again immediately. "It's not for me! I don't drink!"

She shuffles off. The shop assistant glares after her for a moment and very slowly, without blinking, with one hand screws up the piece of paper into a tight ball, rotates her palm and drops the ball onto the floor. It falls in slow motion and silence. For several seconds she's frozen, staring, then she glances at the next customer – me – and pastes on a forced smile. "Next please." I step forward and hand her my pie. I so want to ask how much a bottle of vodka is – and add that it's not for me – it's causing me physical pain not to say it, but I hold it in… because I want to live.

Outside, with the pie stashed in my rucksack for later, I spot a sign for the Cardiff Bay Barrage. That's where I had wanted to aim for anyway. It's about a twenty-minute walk through residential streets. There are terraces and semi-detached houses; varying architecture, varying styles from various periods; the whole area seems very nice, it looks nice, it *feels* nice.

I drop downhill into Penarth Dock. I gaze at the view across Cardiff Bay. The water is very dark, but the sky above is darker. Every building in the Bay seems to be making a statement and is bold and distinctive. I can see the Saint David's Hotel, the first five-star hotel in Wales, with its weird roof adornment, which looks like a giant windsurfer has become entangled in an extractor fan. I stayed here once with Nicky. She is quite into the idea of spa hotels and relaxing. I'm quite *not*. It was a very impressive hotel though with great views across the bay. It opened in 2000, the same time that Cardiff's renowned Millennium Centre *didn't*.

The Millennium Centre had a delayed inception. The first phase of the iconic structure, containing the National Theatre and Arts Centre, opened in 2004. The concept for the building was that it should express "Welshness" and be instantly recognisable, which it certainly is. The materials used come from Wales. The exterior is clad in slate from Welsh quarries. The unmistakable domed roof is clad in steel treated with copper oxide. Most noticeable of all is the writing across the front; a Welsh sentence reads: CREU GWIR FEL GWYDR O FFWRNAIS AWEN, which means 'Creating Truth Like Glass From Inspiration's Furnace'. And an English sentence, the equally poetic or pretentious: IN THESE STONES HORIZONS SING.

The 2005 *Doctor Who* reboot and its spin-off series, *Torchwood*, were filmed at the BBC studios in the Bay. Both made use of the plaza directly in front of the Millennium Centre.

Next door is the late-Victorian, red brick Pierhead Building, in French Gothic Renaissance style. It's very ecclesiastical-looking; it looks like a big, red brick church. This is part of the Welsh National Assembly, known as the "Welsh Big Ben" because of its clock tower.

Cardiff Bay has become a tourist hotspot, built from largely derelict former docklands. This came about in the 1990's when the Cardiff Bay Barrage was constructed to protect the inner bay from the sea, making it essentially a freshwater lake, safe for sailing. The barrage includes a roadway, sections of which can be raised to let shipping traffic through. The barrage was opened to the public in 2001. So pretty much everything in Cardiff Bay is more millennial than the eponymous Millennium Centre.

I watch as six sailing dinghies are tacking steadily across the bay. (I don't know what *tacking* is, I just know it's what yachts do... and yes, I could Google it, but there should be some mysteries in life.)

I trudge my way back uphill through the houses. With my hoodie hood up, wearing my waterproof and being unshaven and a bit grizzly, I look like a vagrant. Or possibly an escaped convict. For once, when people stare and wonder if their homes and families are safe, I don't blame them.

I follow a sign between houses to a viewpoint. There's a great panorama over the seafront and pier of Penarth directly below, and in the not-too-distant distance the islands, one with a lighthouse, Flat Holm, out in the Bristol Channel. In the distant distance in the opposite direction, I can see the white towers and suspension cables of the Second Severn Crossing... or the "new bridge over the River Severn", as it's perhaps more commonly known. Across the water from me is another country. This time that other country is *my* country: England. I love Wales and am in no hurry to cross the border. It's always amazing to have a view like this, which covers so much: two countries, so much sea, so much sky and an iconic feat of engineering. They say from space the only things you can see are the Great Wall of China and the Second Severn Crossing. (I *think* that's what they say. But if the question comes up in a pub quiz use your discretion.)

When I'm leaving Penarth, SatNav Sally's first instruction is again erroneous: "Turn left in 0.1 miles." This would take me off the cliff and into the sea. When I refuse to comply, she changes her mind and instructs me to turn right instead. Good call. I think this is the first time she has ever admitted she was wrong, so it feels like quite a victory.

The journey through and around Cardiff is very tedious. I had hoped I'd just scrape through before the proper rush-hour begins, but I get caught right up in it. I've been to Cardiff several times with Nicky, so I know there's a great old city somewhere in there, but all I see on this occasion is tarmac and the tail lights of the vehicle in front – stationary for most of the time – and the occasional glimpse of the only half-alive areas of characterless, faceless, corporate hotels and office buildings.

I had booked a site earlier by phone. After forking out for the tyre replacement, trying to keep the budget low has gone out of the window. I could have finished Wales today and moved onto the coast that's been opposite me all afternoon, but I've been delaying moving on. But I'll tell you why tomorrow. Maybe.

I eventually arrive at the site. It's nice enough – at least as far as I can tell in the dark. The couple who run it are incredibly friendly. I'm told I can take a pitch near "the lake" if I like. I *do* like. But when I get there, I see the term "lake" is perhaps a bit ambitious, it's definitely only a pond, and a very small pond at that, but still, it's nice.

* * * * * * * * * * *

It's a beautiful sunny morning, but lying in bed with the heater on I'm so cold. I wait for a long time for the van to warm up, which is a bad move, because it doesn't. I give up and get dressed in the cold, by which time the sun has gone. Then I find the reason it's so cold is that one of the windows is wide open and all my heat has been going straight out to do its worst on the ozone layer.

I wish I could say "Time in bed is never time wasted." Probably like Sean Connery, maybe with a suggestive raise of one eyebrow, ("Time in bed is never time wasted, Moneypenny.") but I feel my time in bed this morning was very wasted. To make matters worse, everyone else on the site is up and out; it's popular with people working in Cardiff and migrant workers on the farms apparently... which makes me feel like a waster.

I set off along the M4. I come off at Junction 2, to have a look at Chepstow, which sounds quaint. I park in the shadow of the magnificent castle, which was ordered by William the Conqueror, considered to be the oldest surviving English-built castle, though Will was hardly English, having only just invaded the land and conquered it, hence his name.

I thought Chepstow was in England – it sounds so

English. As a result, I put on my Union Jack hoodie again, because at this stage all my other clothes are only fit for burning. It turns out Chepstow is in fact in Monmouthshire, Wales. I quickly put my fleece over the top of the blaring Union Jack, lest I be run out of town at a rapid saunter.

I walk around the castle. (You can walk around most of the outside for free or pay to go inside. Guess which I chose.) In the parkland at the rear of the castle, two scallies in jogging pants and baseball caps come swaggering gansta-stylee towards a third identical clone, innit. Something changes hands, man, then they all slope off together, doing a skanky, arm-swinging walk that's so forced and unnatural it's really comical. They look like they're going for a stroll in zero gravity and are leaving a lingering, grey trail of hash smoke behind them. Either that, or they've singed a kipper.

The centre of Chepstow is very nice. The local businesses have gone for the old personal name thing in a big way: Mikes News, (sic – no apostrophe) Hannah's Music, Luke's Barbershop and Neptune Laundry Service. (I'm not sure it actually belongs to Neptune himself though.) I pass colourful little painted cottages on lovely steep streets, cobbled lanes and stone flag pavements. Chepstow is a charming town.

I'm really hungry; I try to resist the pangs, but resistance is futile, so I call into a nice pub and order a half of Peroni and vegetarian sausages on a bed of mash with peas and a rich red onion gravy. It's really tasty, especially the gravy. (They're garden peas. Being northern, I prefer mushy peas, but I'm prepared to rough it when I have to.) The pub staff are really friendly. I make up my mind that if the bar maid calls me "lovely" once more – "Alright, lovely?", "Did you enjoy it, lovely?", "Thank you, lovely." then I'm going to marry her. It's amazing how suddenly she stops saying it.

After I've eaten, I have another wander around the quaint old town. I do a bit of charity shop worrying. A sign outside one says URGENT VOLUNTEERS NEEDED. The two old folks currently volunteering are anything but urgent. I wonder how they managed to get through the rigorous screening process. The poor chap behind the till is just staring into space, as he probably does every other day at home, but he comes in here once a week just to stare into a different portion of space.

Chepstow is very picturesque, quaint and charming. Let's do the test: could I live here, would I live here, should I live here? Yes, yes, yes... I think *so!*

* * * * * * * * * * *

I have one final location to visit in Wales. The sun has come out again as I'm driving the short distance to the village of Beachley, which sits on the banks of the River Severn, close to where the original Severn Bridge crosses from Wales to England.

The area is home to an MOD establishment, a training school, and many of the houses and buildings belong to them. There are a lot of chain-link fences around and severe warning signs to KEEP OUT. I keep out and park in the shadow of the bridge, which strides over the river. It's *huge*; the tallest thing for miles. It completely dominates the landscape.

The Severn Bridge took three-and-a-half years to build and cost £8 million. It was opened in 1966, by the Queen. #1 It is quite rightly a Grade I listed building. Currently, a toll is charged to cross *into* Wales, but not to *leave* Wales, so it has been heavily criticised as being a "tax on Wales". There are plans afoot to abolish the toll in the very near future.

I go for a potter along the Severn's stony beach. The sun is so bright that the cars crossing the bridge are just dazzling specks. The noise when larger vehicles go over is deafening, like a roll of thunder. This is a feat of engineering, the size, the scale, the achievement, and the aesthetic quality. This is iconic and breath-taking to look at.

I can just see the other bridge, the "new bridge", in the distance, shining in the sunlight. The Second Severn Crossing was opened in 1996 by Prince Charles. It's just over three miles in length compared to the mile-long "old bridge". At high tide there can be up to 14 metres of water beneath it.

My attention is on the bridge, which is towering above me, so I'm not fully looking where I'm going – I nearly step on something; in my peripheral vision it looks exactly like a body. It gives me a real jolt. Time stops. So do I. The body – the former person – seems to have their limbs splayed as though they've fallen from the bridge. They are wearing some sort of beige clothing. I get all this information in less than a second without even looking directly at it. I leap back, my heart racing. I stare in horror and disbelief... at the log. It's the bough of a tree with branches coming off that look like limbs. On top of it is a neatly placed beige jacket, that possibly someone has dropped. From these objects, my mind has conjured up quite a different image, most probably because this is a sight you may be unfortunate enough to see here or at Beachy Head, so your mind is filling in the gaps. I'm quite shaken, which is stupid, but I have to retreat to Eagle One and have a piece of rhubarb pie. That does the trick.

(Note to self: First Aid kit – in addition to plasters, sterile wipes, antiseptic, bandages etc – to be augmented with a rhubarb pie: to be administered for stress and anxiety.)

Out in the strong, tidal waters of the Severn, SARA, the Severn Area Rescue Association are doing exercises in power boats. They seem to be an all-male crew today. They are circling around the giant supports of the bridge, as you might do if you were looking for a weighed-down body.

The Severn Bridge has a reputation as a suicide hotspot. This is the last confirmed location of Richey Edwards from the Manic Street Preachers, who disappeared on 1st February 1995. Richey, along with his three bandmates, grew up in Blackwood, Caerphilly, a former mining town, not too far from here. Edwards became a fashion icon with a horde of adoring followers. He suffered from severe depression and famously self-harmed, including cutting the words 4 REAL into his arm with a razor blade in front of a horrified journalist.

In the two weeks before he went missing, Richey withdrew £200 a day from his bank account, amounting to £2,800. He disappeared from a London hotel and drove to his apartment in Cardiff, after which the trail grew cold, except for several alleged sightings, including at a passport office, a bus station and by a taxi driver who supposedly picked him up and drove him around the valleys, including Blackwood. He was subsequently dropped off at the Severn View service station on the English side of the river.

Just over a week later, Richey's Vauxhall Cavalier was reported as abandoned at the same services. The battery was dead and the car was filled with food refuse, as though it had been lived in. Due to the service station's proximity to the Severn Bridge, it was assumed he had jumped to his death. Since then, like Elvis, he has "been spotted" all over the world, though none of the sightings have been conclusive.

In 2008, it was announced that Richey had been declared dead in absentia. #2

* * * * * * * * * * *

I leave Wales at some point – it's quite unceremonious because I don't see a sign. #3 I'm meandering through the Wye valley in slanting late afternoon sun, between freshly ploughed fields and autumn hedgerows.

Now is the time – I can't put it off any longer – I have to share something with you, dear friend. I'm going home. I've kept something from you, because I know we've grown close and I didn't want you to get upset, but my beautiful van, Eagle One, has some serious issues regarding structural integrity. There are a few other problems as well, such as the intermittent loss of power when accelerating and possibly an alternator issue. Oh and the meshing on gears 2 and 5. Oh, and the water ingress over the cab section... I'll stop there. I've been told my van won't pass her MOT in January and that there is no way to repair all the structural issues safely, however, Ewan the mechanic the other day had a different opinion.

I have reluctantly decided to close this section of the trip for now. I've done the Northwest of England and all of Wales, so it feels like a suitable place for a hiatus. I suppose it was stupid to start in the bleakest season, but that was mainly down to my dad being ill that my start date kept getting put back. Anyway, I'm heading home for Christmas and I will look into getting Eagle One, my van, my mobile hub, sorted or replaced.

I'd like to thank you for joining me – you've been a great travelling companion. Have a good Christmas, all the best for the New Year and I really hope that as the worst of the frosts thaw next year, we're underway again, starting from the Severn Bridge.

* * * * * * * * * *

If Brendan was with me...

Brendan would probably have coped well with south Wales, though I may well have been put off going in cafes and pubs. He is generally much better with people nowadays, but you never can tell and sometimes someone will annoy him for some unfathomable reason, like they're wearing a cardigan he doesn't approve of, and he'll start barking at them.

I loved this trip. I enjoyed it so much. If Brendan had

been with me it would certainly have been different, but just having him by my side could only have made it even better.

ABOVE: Me in Eagle One. She's bigger on the inside.

NOTES

#1: Of course, since writing this, the Queen - by which I mean Queen Elizabeth II - has died and been succeeded by her son, Prince Charles, AKA King Charles III. For most people they had only known one monarch, and that was the Queen. When she died it was a "Kennedy moment" - everyone remembers where they were when they heard the news. We - that's Brendan and I - were on holiday meeting my schoolfriend Paul in Wiltshire, as we do every year. We were in a pub having our evening meal (mushroom risotto) when the landlord announced it. Although it was expected, it was strangely surreal and somehow deadening.

#2: As of 2023, there has still been no discovery of the whereabouts of Richey Edwards, or a body.

#3: I was planning to stay the night in a car park close to the Severn Crossing, which I had read on a website accepted overnight parking. In the end I chose not to; I had a black dog on my shoulder that night. I was sorry that the trip was coming to an untimely end, and the dark notoriety of the bridge and my mind lodged on Richey Edwards put me off; I just wanted to get further away. Instead I spent a relaxing night in the depths of the Wye Forest.

ABOVE & BELOW: The Millennium Centre, Cardiff Bay – by day and night.

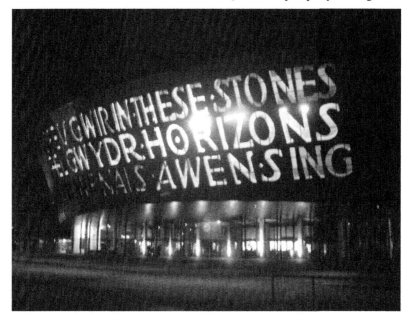

AFTERWORD

I had wanted a complete life change. I thought this trip would show me the way ahead. I half expected to find my new life on my travels and end up collecting seaweed or becoming a tour guide or a weasel whisperer or something like that. I thought I'd learn things about myself; there's nothing like being alone to expose your weaknesses. And what I learned is that I know myself pretty well, and I came back the same person.

Thinking back about this trip I have many fond memories, though it wasn't all plain sailing. I had to make some tough decisions: "There's only one teabag left... do I have it now or later?" There were hardships: "This towel's still wet from this morning!" There were compromises: "There's only an apple pie, and I wanted rhubarb!" Such is life on the road. But I did learn that very few problems cannot be either solved or considerably eased by having a cup of tea and a piece of cake. I also learned that in the absence of cake a pie will suffice. And the aforementioned Co-op rhubarb pie had got me out of a few sticky scrapes.

So, what happened next? Well, I went home for Christmas and arranged for a mammoth restoration operation to be carried out on my van, including a lot of welding and undersealing. My Dad became ill and went into hospital, then a respite home. He was never expected to recover or come out of the home – but he did. During this time Nicky decided we would volunteer at an animal sanctuary, and there we met Brendan. He walked into the room, climbed onto the settee where we were sitting and went to sleep.

And that's where our book *underdogs* begins.

As much as I had enjoyed this trip, once I got Brendan, this first solo leg of the journey was overlooked and archived really, because I thought who would be interested in it when it doesn't feature Brendan? However, I reread it recently prior to junking it and I found – to my great surprise – that even though Brendan was missing with his funny ways and his demanding behaviour – I found it really interesting and amusing and I didn't want to waste it. So here it is, delivered to you as a prequel to *underdogs.* It was a great and memorable experience. Little did I know then that the best was yet to come.

MY LOVE OF CAMPERVANS

Travelling around in a van has its own special joy for me. Basically, I'm driving round with my own curtains and at any moment I can close them and shut out the world. Never being more than an arms-length away from the kettle is also something of a major plus-point. That said, I used to really enjoy going into cafes and pubs, relaxing with an Americano and watching the world go by. These days though, with my dog Brendan in tow, I generally prefer staying in my van, so I don't have to apologise to people for my dog frightening them, barking at them or issuing ransom demands for their children.

As we get older, do we really get more like our parents? For many years it was my dad's dream to own a campervan. When I was in my late teens, Dad finally got his wish and bought a little classic VW. For their first trip they decided to go to the Lake District. Although I was too old to be going on holiday with my parents, I leapt on board at the prospect of a free ride up to the Lakes. I slept in my tent with our family dog, Gemma, and spent the days walking.

Over the years, Mum and Dad upgraded frequently, getting larger and larger vans. The difference between a campervan and a motorhome is generally the on-board facilities. A motorhome literally has everything in, bathroom, showers, microwave, TV, heating, slippers, and a full range of tinned soups.

Mum and Dad joined a rally association, where motorhome owners would meet up at odd places, like industrial estates and school playgrounds out of term time, park in a circle, have barbeques and go in and out of each other's vans admiring their cupboard doors and whimsical tea towels. There was something potentially swinger-ish about it, but I'm sure it was all above board.

My own personal first-hand experience of campervan life was when I borrowed Mum and Dad's first big van and went to Wales with my schoolfriend, Paul. It was like a proper roadtrip, the sun was shining, we had music playing, we were singing away, we had our walking boots and Paul had brought his suit. It was the Eighties and people did things like that. Some people did anyway.

On our first night, we parked on the Menai Straits and I remember – as though it was yesterday – the thrill of being in this fabulous location, but with all the comforts of home. We ate our tea – lasagne – looking out over the slate-blue of the Straits. It was amazing. We were in Wales... but we were also at home! I can't describe the thrill. And that thrill has never left me.

People often ask me: "Does your partner, Nicky, go away in your van with you?" The answer is no. The answer is never. It's never, EVER going to happen. To her, spending the night in a van would be the worst sort of punishment. She would rather spend a night in prison, where at least they have toilets and hot and cold running water. So, while I'm on my next trip with Brendan, I've arranged for her to spend the weekend in Holloway.

ABOVE: My beautiful van, Eagle One.

BELOW: Our new van... as yet unnamed.

ABOVE: Room with a view. This is what I love about the idea of vanlife and van travel; you park somewhere and you have a new view, yet your home is still with you. This is near Pwellheli on the Llyn Peninsula and this is the view I woke up to. I used to spend nights "off the beaten track" a lot before I got Brendan. With Brendan - as far as I can recall - I've only had one stay that wasn't on a site, and that was because we had broken down and spent several nights on an industrial estate in Portishead. Brendan barked all night and there were burglar alarms and allsorts of disturbances. It wasn't the best experience. (See *underdogs* for the full story.)

MY LOVE OF LIGHTHOUSES

I love lighthouses. This trip was originally all about visiting every lighthouse in England and Wales. And that's what I did.

I can trace my fascination with lighthouses back to my childhood, when I first read *Moominpappa at Sea.* (I'm being serious!) Those shy but endearing hippo-like Scandinavians travel to a remote island and live there in a lighthouse. I'd love to live in a lighthouse; imagine the peace, the solitude. I love the isolated locations of many of the best lighthouses, where the only dwelling is the lighthouse-keeper's cottage; where the only light is the steady blinking of the lighthouse beam; where the only sounds are the tortured cries of the seagulls... and the metaphors.

Wales, in particular, has some amazing lighthouses. Two of my favourites are South Stack, for its architecture and dramatic setting, and Trywn Du for its atmosphere and location, opposite Puffin Island.

This book was originally to be called *Coasting* and was all about lighthouses. When rereading it recently, I realised the whole of the emphasis of the book has changed. It's no longer a journey visiting lighthouses – it's a journey I made directly before meeting my dog, Brendan. It is a journey I made alone, without him. Suddenly, all the lighthouse stuff seemed irrelevant, so I edited most of it out. So it's gone. But I still love lighthouses and have now visited every one in England and Wales and they still thrill me.

Lighthouses: Happisburgh,
Norfolk; Hurst Point, Hampshire;
Beachy Head, Sussex.

Lighthouses: Trwyn Du, Anglesey;
Longstone, Farne Islands; Godrevy,
Cornwall.

ALSO BY GRAY FREEMAN

underdogs

underdogs is the story of a man and a dog who meet when they most need each other. It is an autobiography, a travelogue, an adventure, a voyage of discovery. It is uplifting, touching, heart-warming and hilariously funny. It's Wallace and Gromit with an axe to grind in a campervan.

"Brendan was a street dog. He ran all day through the cobbled alleyways of Bulgaria, scavenging, possibly busking, probably scamming tourists."

Gray likes walking, travelling and exploring new places; Brendan likes staying at home, watching daytime TV and weeing on trees. Despite this, they embark on a - sometime idyllic, sometimes disastrous - roadtrip around Britain, to acquaint Brendan with his new homeland.

"Brendan had baggage. He'd had a hard life and was afraid of almost everything, including men, women, uniforms and anyone carrying anything, such as a stick, a bag or a grudge."

underdogs is about a human and canine bond. It's about taking a chance and trying to live your dream.

DOG DAYS:
underdogs II

Finding they were unable to return to a life on the road as the coronavirus cast its black shadow over the world, Gray and Brendan decided to use the time to try and improve themselves, and – most importantly – to try and find positivity in every day. This began well, but it wasn't long before their world started to fall apart.

Dog Days is a diary of that unprecedented period in history. It is in turns touching, funny, optimistic, poignant, tragic and very human. Despite everything going wrong in the world, *Dog Days* is about the joy of spending every second of every day with your best friend.

The Long Goodbye
& Other Plays

NOTHING IS AS IT SEEMS.

The Long Goodbye was a play. It was staged twice in Manchester. People laughed, people cried, people said how much they could relate to it. You will also be able to relate to it. It is funny, tragic and touching; it leaves a lasting impression.

WAKE UP AND A WHOLE NEW LIFE HAS BEEN WRITTEN FOR YOU – A LIFE WHICH YOU KNOW MUST BE A LIE.

The Long Goodbye made a humorous, moving and memorable piece of theatre, and here it is presented as a "reading script" – between a script and a novel. It is accessible, at times laugh-out-loud funny and also deeply poignant. On the page it doesn't lose any of its humour or haunting impact.

EVERYTHING IS BIZARRE AND SURREAL, LIKE A 'SIXTIES TV SHOW. YOUR LIFE IS A PRISON; YOU ARE THE PRISONER.

AND FINALLY... A NOTE FROM THE AUTHOR

Thank you for buying and reading this book. I am so grateful. I hope you have enjoyed it. Please consider putting a review on Amazon – it makes such a difference.

Stay safe and enjoy your own travels!

Checkout our Facebook page: https://www.facebook.com/BrendanFreedog

Thanks to Nicky Lambert for the cover shot and additional photos.

Thanks to the Knowhere Guide for much hilarity!

This book is dedicated to the memory of Brendan's brother, Hector, who has gone to join his sister, but who hasn't really gone away at all.

Printed in Great Britain
by Amazon